5/7

D1549130

indoor gardening
the organic way

indoor gardening the organic way

How to Create a Natural and Sustaining Environment for Your Houseplants

Julie Bawden-Davis

Illustrations by
Sabrina Rose Davis
Photographs by Chas Metivier

taylor trade publishing
Lanham • New York • Boulder • Toronto • Plymouth, UK

Copyright © 2007 by Julie Bawden-Davis
First Taylor Trade Publishing edition 2007

This Taylor Trade Publishing paperback edition of *Indoor Gardening the Organic Way*
is an original publication. It is published by arrangement with the author.

All rights reserved. No part of this book may be reproduced in any form or by any
electronic or mechanical means, including information storage and retrieval
systems, without written permission from the publisher, except by a reviewer
who may quote passages in a review.

Published by Taylor Trade Publishing
An imprint of The Rowman & Littlefield Publishing Group, Inc.
4501 Forbes Boulevard, Suite 200, Lanham, Maryland 20706

Estover Road, Plymouth PL6 7PY, United Kingdom

Distributed by NATIONAL BOOK NETWORK

Library of Congress Cataloging-in-Publication Data

Bawden-Davis, Julie.
    Indoor gardening the organic way : how to create a natural and sustaining
environment for your houseplants / Julie Bawden-Davis.—1st Taylor Trade
Publishing ed.
       p. cm.
    Includes bibliographical references and index.
    ISBN-13: 978-1-58979-293-7 (pbk. : alk. paper)
    ISBN-10: 1-58979-293-9 (pbk. : alk. paper)
    1. Indoor gardening. 2. Organic gardening. I. Title. II. Title: How to
create a natural and sustaining environment for your houseplants.

  SB419.B235 2007
  635.9'65—dc22

                                                          2006021537

∞™The paper used in this publication meets the minimum requirements of
American National Standard for Information Sciences—Permanence of
Paper for Printed Library Materials, ANSI/NISO Z39.48-1992.

Manufactured in the United States of America.

contents

indoor gardening the organic way

acknowledgments

I am grateful to Brooke Taggart of Plant'It Earth for her guidance during the writing of this book. The seeds for the concept of gardening indoors organically were planted during our conversations over the years. I would also like to thank my daughter, Sabrina, for helping to create the book I envisioned by drawing such beautiful illustrations, my sons, Danny and Jeremy, for their helpfulness and patience during the long writing process, and my husband, Greg, who always understands my vision and constantly supports and encourages my writing dreams.

introduction

When I began writing my houseplant column, "The Gardener Within," in 1997, gardening organically outdoors had become the norm. If I asked horticulturists about natural gardening indoors, however, I always got a resounding *no*. They would tell me to leave organic gardening to the outside. This whole idea puzzled me. Why could we live a healthy, natural lifestyle, yet not do the same for our foliage friends? How could it be okay for us to eat organic produce and clean our indoor air while at the same time polluting it with harsh synthetic chemical fertilizers and pesticides?

For health reasons, I began experimenting with organic gardening indoors. What soon astounded me was how readily my houseplants responded to a natural diet and less invasive pesticide treatments. They looked healthier than I'd ever seen them. Some plants that had never fruited or flowered began doing so, and I got multiple compliments on my indoor garden.

I sometimes hear from people who feed their plants synthetic chemical fertilizers that their indoor gardens are doing just great. All I can say is, what if your garden could be even better? Gardening indoors organically is healthy for you and your plants.

Remember that you are Mother or Father Nature to your houseplants. You manipulate the environment they live in and allow them to grow strong or falter. The organic principles in this book teach you how to grow your plants as nature intended so that you can enjoy a lush indoor garden paradise.

indoor gardening the organic way

I

choose your foliage friends carefully and make them feel at home

Houseplants enter this life much like we do. In order to get them to a sufficient size and shape for growing on their own, they must be carefully planted, coddled, and coaxed to grow big and strong. In many ways the greenhouse where this birthing process takes place is a lot like a mother's womb. In these climate-controlled, warm humidity chambers, plants are consistently fed with nutrient-rich water. They're even sprayed with growth hormones, which accelerate their transformation into big, marketable plants, or growth retardants to avoid an upward sprawl. Add to this that the levels of CO_2 on which plants thrive are elevated in greenhouses as a byproduct of heating them—and are sometimes even pumped with extra gas to move growth along—and you've got plant paradise.

The good life doesn't last forever, though. Once the

When they're ready for sale, houseplants make a long, stressful journey to plant suppliers.

young plants grow to a sufficient size, they're thrown into the real world, where temperature, light, and humidity extremes are common. Growers yank them from their feeding tubes, separating them from their brothers and sisters, and pot them up individually. Placed in dark containers and flung onto trucks, they make a shaky voyage to a distribution center. Because many are grown in California, Florida, and Hawaii, this journey can take up to two weeks, depending on their destination. Upon arrival, they're split up and sent out to nurseries and home and garden centers where they are displayed in hopes of enticing a potential owner. This is where you, the plant's surrogate parent, come in. If the plant catches your eye, you take it home to live the good life with you. How you treat your new offspring in its first few weeks can greatly affect its chances for a healthy life.

indoor gardening the organic way

Acclimating a plant to your home requires keeping a few things in mind. Your first order of business is to detox the plant from synthetic food and growth hormones. Unless the greenhouse where your plant was raised is an organic one (most aren't), your new addition was fed a continuous supply of chemical fertilizers and sprayed with artificial growth hormones.

While the "fast food" your plant has come to rely on did encourage foliage growth, it did nothing to nurture the soil and very little to develop strong roots. Chances are the soil is devoid of the beneficial soil microbes and fungi needed for full, sustained growth and may have a build-up of soluble salts, which can lead to a variety of problems, including leaf burn and drop. One of the best things you can do for a newly arrived plant, even if it doesn't appear to need it, is to repot it with a nutrient-rich organic soil. Repotting will enable the plant to immediately build up beneficial soil microorganisms and develop strong sustaining roots (see chapters 2 and 9). At the very least, leach out chemical fertilizers and accumulated salts and repot as soon as you can (see chapter 3).

Withdrawal from the synthetic steroids applied to your plants in the form of growth hormones is also likely to occur. Avoid shock by applying a liquid seaweed fertilizer to the soil and on the leaves as a foliar spray (one brand is Maxicrop). Products containing seaweed are a natural, organic form of the cytokinins found in synthetic growth hormones.

I also suggest giving your plants a vitamin B1 mix such

as Superthrive, which studies have shown helps reduce shock and encourage adjustment. Such products also contain other vitamins and various hormones.

A ROOM OF THEIR OWN

Make your plant's homecoming a success by providing the ideal environment upon arrival. A well-matched location will help prevent shock and encourage new growth. Consult this book's encyclopedia to determine the best spot in terms of lighting and humidity. Dracaenas, for instance, will do well in an indirect light area, while *Ficus benjamina* needs a bright home. Your arrowhead vine (*Syngonium podophyllum*) may look great in front of a south-facing bay window at first, but it doesn't like bright light and will yellow and burn. Place plants that like 60% humidity and above on humidity trays as soon as they arrive and keep the spray bottle handy as they adapt to their new surroundings. When choosing plants, remember that it's best to bring home selections that most closely match your home environment.

THE PICK OF THE CROP

Of course, this is all assuming that you bring home a healthy plant in the first place. Keep your indoor garden in top form by being discriminating about who you introduce to your foliage family. A sick plant can wreak havoc on the rest of your collection, so make sure new introductions are robust. Once a plant is ill, returning it to a healthy state can

making the move

Whether you're moving existing plants or bringing new foliage family members home, keep in mind that they may react badly to relocating. Houseplants tend to be fragile and temperamental when it comes to changing spaces. When moving is a must, keep the following tips in mind:

1. So that your plants aren't overly heavy with water on moving day, schedule watering for arrival. During periods of high heat, water enough to moisten plants. For the last two or three waterings before moving day, help prevent shock by using a B-1 solution.

2. Crumple newspaper and tape it to the top of the pot so that you don't lose soil. Or, if you'll be moving the plants in hot weather, wet sphagnum moss and secure to the soil surface.

3. Tie big plants up with green garden tape as much as possible to keep the limbs from flopping and breaking. Place them on their side when transporting.

4. Always lift plants by their containers—never by the plant itself.

5. Remember that your plants are used to mild indoor temperatures and aren't accustomed to or even designed to be out in the ele-

ments. Houseplants should always be transported in an enclosed vehicle and kept away from direct sun, heat, and extreme cold. Throwing plants in the back of an open pickup truck is equivalent to putting them into the middle of a hurricane. Even in mild weather, they'll get windburn and sunburn and reach their desti-

(continued)

Wrap small- and medium-sized plants before transporting them.

nation a torn-up mess. Protect your investment when it comes to large plants and consider having them delivered. Leaving plants unattended inside of a car on a hot or cold day is also unadvisable (remember, they're like infants!). Even a short amount of time in extreme temperatures will kill or severely damage a plant. Protect small- and medium-sized plants by wrapping them in paper (high-quality plant retailers will do this for you when you purchase a plant).

6. Expect an adjustment period. Depending on how traumatic the journey home was, it may take a while for a plant to grow accustomed to its new space.

be challenging, and the chance of infecting other plants is high. Do keep in mind, however, that you might bring home a plant that looks healthy only to watch it go downhill. While many would-be gardeners lament black thumbs, the fact is that some plants are set up to fail. Houseplants that finish their long journey from the greenhouse and arrive at a retail establishment only to be mistreated through improper watering and inappropriate light often contract pest and disease problems, which usually don't manifest themselves for several weeks—often after you've brought them home. If possible, return the plant and demand a refund.

SIGNS OF HEALTH
What to Look For

To choose a healthy plant, look for the following:

- New growth that is firm, thriving, and normal in size and shape. This new growth is a much better indicator of current plant health than old growth.

indoor gardening the organic way

choosing and assessing your plant source

In general, nurseries, specialty garden centers, greenhouses, arboretums, and botanic gardens do the best job of caring for houseplants because they're experts and have a reputation to uphold. Purchase a houseplant at an arboretum plant sale, for instance, and you're likely to buy directly from the grower. While major chain home and garden centers often carry a good supply of indoor plants, they may not have the proper facilities, which can mean mishandled plants. They are also likely to lack trained personnel to care for them and answer your questions. This is not to say that you can't ever find a good houseplant at a large home and garden store; there are definitely exceptions. Your best bet is to carefully assess the plant source and trust your instincts. Look at the health of the plants overall. Do they look robust and well tended? Also examine the turnover rate. (This takes visiting several times.) Do the plants get bought and move out quickly, or do they tend to stay around? Also look at light to water ratio. Plants in bright light that are moist are probably okay, but plants in low light that are soggy may already have a fungal pathogen. If you are uncertain of how plants are treated at a particular location, ask when they get their deliveries and go in when the plants are fresh off the truck. You'll get the best pick of the bunch.

- Flower buds and new flowers.
- A plant that is well anchored in the soil.
- Fairly uniform rich color throughout the plant and vibrant-looking leaves.
- Abundant white, firm roots. (Some plant roots are covered with an outer casing that is brown, but once removed should expose sturdy white or slightly tan roots.)

A healthy plant looks vigorous and vibrant.

• A plant that looks contented. Your instincts will tell you if a plant is doing well. It will stand or hang well and its leaves will have a healthy sheen.

What to Avoid

Steer clear of plants that display the following symptoms:

- Droopy, wilted leaves, despite wet soil; reduced, distorted, shriveled, or overly soft new growth; fungus on the leaves or at the base of the plant. These are signs that a plant is suffering from a bacterial or fungal infection of its roots that prevents it from taking up water. Brown, squishy, even smelly roots are also a sign of infection.
- Pot-bound plants with a mass of tangled, encircling roots. Such plants have been deprived of sufficient nutrients and possibly water.
- Wobbly base; a houseplant that appears to be loosely rooted has root rot or has been injured and roots have been severed. Either way, the plant is not likely to fare well.
- Leaf tip browning, which indicates that the plant has been subjected to overly dry conditions.

indoor gardening the organic way

- An obvious stunting and failure to thrive.
- Legginess; stretching or leaning to one side. These indicate inadequate light.
- Unnaturally large leaves and stems. Oftentimes plants given excessive amounts of CO_2 or growth hormones will have an elongated look to the leaves and stems that don't mesh with the plant overall. While many plants are given some growth hormones and it's possible to wean them from such treatment, excessive amounts may mean the plant will never look or be quite right.
- Sticky residue on plant leaves or around pot—a sign of pests.
- Yellow, curling, chlorotic leaves and foliage loss, which indicates a possible nutrient deficiency, pest, or that underwatering has occurred.
- Plants that have had leaf shine applied, which will clog pores and compromise the plant's health.
- Visible pests. Houseplants fall victim to a few indoor troublemakers, including aphids, mealybugs, spider mites, thrips, and scale (see chapter 8). Thoroughly check the entire plant with a magnifying glass or 10× hand lens. Look closely at the top and bottom of leaves, in all cracks and crevices, including the leaf axils—where the leaves meet the stem—and in new leaves that have yet to unfurl.

you've got mail and it's alive

Garden indoors long enough and you'll tire of the more common house-plants and gravitate toward the exotic and unusual. Although local nurseries sometimes carry offbeat plants, they often lack the space or personnel to consistently stock a wide variety. Open up a catalog that carries houseplants, though, and you'll discover a captivating world. There are plants with un-usual foliage, fragrant plants, small terrarium plants, and rare specimens. Shopping via mail-order is a great way to add spark to your indoor garden. Though it's a little disconcerting to purchase a plant sight unseen, many on-line companies have pictures and descriptions, and most offer a money-back guarantee.

Keep the following tips in mind when ordering indoor plants through the mail:

1. Be realistic. Realize that the plant examples pictured in the catalog or online are photographed at peak times. The plants you order via mail will probably require some growing time before they become as showy. Many plants will come quite small and may need a year or more to mature.

2. Check on timing. Make sure that you will be home or nearby on the day your plants are expected. Avoid having them sit outdoors in extreme weather.

3. Open immediately. Check for a packing slip and make certain your order is intact and in good shape. Call with any concerns or complaints.

4. Soak plants upon arrival. If the plants come without pots, hydrate them after their long journey by soaking them in water for 8 to 12 hours. Soak just the roots, leaving the foliage above water, and then pot them up. Plants in soil should be thoroughly moistened.

TEMPORARY QUARANTINE

Even when a plant appears healthy, once you get it home, it's a good idea to keep it isolated for two to three weeks, during which time you can watch for latent pests or disease.

PLANTS ARE RESILIENT

Have patience and compassion for the new additions to your foliar family. Realize that after their abrupt introduction into the world and bumpy journey to your home, they'll be feeling down for a little while. Though they may respond to their new quarters with some leaf drop, with a little TLC they'll soon snap out of it and resume growth.

2

it's all in the soil

If there's one adage that indoor gardeners should remember, it's this: Never treat your soil like dirt. Although we tend to focus on plants, the health of the soil is really the most critical ingredient because plant roots live in it. Roots may not be the prettiest part of the plant, but they are its life force. Without healthy roots, you will not have a healthy plant. Care for the soil, and you care for the roots, which leads to a thriving indoor garden.

So much goes on inside soil that we know very little about: There's a wild party going on down in our potted plants. In the garden, a single spade of earth contains more species of organisms than can be found in the entire Amazon rainforest. While your potted soil won't be quite so biologically active, it can and should still be as alive as you can make it. As a matter of fact, your potted plants are dependent on you to make their soil the "in" place to be. Instead of putting them in a sterile mix that provides empty calories and requires massive doses of "fast food" chemical fertilizer to keep the plant growing, create a sustaining "health food" soil that mimics nature and provides for the roots and the plant on a continuous basis. You'll be rewarded with vibrant plants that fight off pests and diseases and need less fertilizing.

A healthy soil contains a high degree of beneficial organisms, such as bacteria and fungi. It's these millions of microorganisms living in the soil that accomplish a number of critical tasks, including digesting and converting various raw materials, such as fertilizer, into a form that plants can then absorb through their roots.

HUMUS IS THE SECRET

One major key to creating a rich, active soil for your houseplants is humus. This soft brown-black substance forms in the last stages of decomposition of vegetable or animal matter and is the lifeblood of nature. Rich in nutrients and organic matter, humus creates an environment that supports and encourages beneficial soil bacteria and fungi. It has the amazing ability to simultaneously hold moisture and increase drainage—two contrary but necessary requirements of all houseplants. It also helps plants absorb nutrients more efficiently by making various minerals more readily available. We can thank humus for all of our forests and jungles. This rich organic substance is the reason wild plants grow on their own without outside help like pre-packaged fertilizer. Of course, your potted plants require human intervention. They're depending on you to mimic nature, and humus is one of the best ways to do that.

MULCH ADO ABOUT SOMETHING

One quick and easy way to kick up the humic volume in your houseplant soil is to mulch. Although this is often suggested for houseplants as a way to beautify potted plants by hiding the soil, it's actually extremely beneficial for your indoor plants. Mulching and the resulting decomposition of organic matter lead to the constant production of humus. Mulch also protects important soil organisms and increases the disease resistance of your plants. According to recent research, microorganisms in mulch produce enzymes and other chemicals that stimulate plants to develop systemic acquired resistance (SAR) to some plant diseases. Mulch also shelters the soil from temperature variations common in homes, often from room to room. The more constant the soil temperature, the healthier and happier your soil and plants will be. Mulch also cuts down on watering by as much as 50 to 60%, leaving you free to relax and enjoy your houseplants! When I started to mulch a couple of years ago, my watering chores were easily cut in half. Some plants respond so well to mulch and keep moist with its protective influence, I'm often amazed at how long they go between waterings.

When you apply mulch, you're simulating what occurs in nature. In the forest, the ground is littered with fallen vegetation that insulates and feeds the trees and other

cover me, please

Mulch is an easy way to pump up soil fertility. Here are several organic mulches to choose from:

Chipped or Shredded Bark
Upside: It is attractive and decorative, decomposes slowly, and is especially beneficial for acid loving plants. *Downside:* It may harbor pests such as earwigs and may also compete for nitrogen in the soil. Fertilize with a good nitrogen source such as guano. Mushrooms are also a by-product of composting bark. Eliminate them by topdressing the mulch with dolomite lime.

Coconut Coir
Upside: Made from coconut husks, this is a more sustainable and less environmentally damaging product than peat moss. It tends to have more airspace than peat moss and holds the space a year or more longer. It is naturally rich with beneficial microbes and makes a great soil conditioner. It is also slightly acidic. *Downside:* Will resist wetting if allowed to dry out. If it dries out, water the plant from the bottom by soaking, making sure the coir is thoroughly re-moistened.

Cocoa Mulch™
This is a relatively new mulch that is a natural by-product derived from the cocoa plant. *Upside:* It has a pleasant chocolate aroma and is lightweight, attractive, and easy to spread. It also adds nitrogen, phosphorus, and potassium to the soil (3-1-3). *Downside:* Because it is lightweight, it may wash down the drain when watering over the sink.

plants. There are two main categories of mulch: plant-derived organic types and inorganic mulches. While both keep soil temperatures stable and conserve water, only organic mulch improves soil health.

If you are an indoor gardener who also gardens outdoors, you may already have a compost pile. In that case, take a spade-full indoors and treat your houseplants! If

Cocoa mulch also contains high levels of theobromine, which is toxic to dogs.

Homemade or Bagged Compost
Upside: This is an excellent soil improver. It is an attractive dark, crumbly material that is easy to buy or make by combining organic materials found in the yard and kitchen, such as grass clippings, leaves, shredded branches, and produce scraps. *Downside:* It must be composted properly to avoid weeds, which means the compost pile should reach 140°F.

Leaves
Upside: They are readily available from the outdoors or can be purchased as a bagged product. They decompose fairly quickly, improving the soil once they decay. *Downside:* They may mat and interfere with water and air movement. Avoid this problem by shredding new leaves and letting them age for two weeks before using.

Moss
Upside: Moss is decorative and breaks down slowly, constantly improving the soil. *Downside:* It can inhibit circulation, so place moss loosely on soil to maintain some air circulation.

Peat Moss
Upside: It acidifies houseplant soil, which some plants like. *Downside:* It resists wetting once dry. If it dries out, water the plant from the bottom by soaking, making sure the moss is thoroughly re-moistened. Its harvest also has an adverse environmental impact on peat bogs.

WORM CASTINGS
Upside: Rich in micronutrients, which act as a slow release fertilizer, this will energize the soil. *Downside:* They can dry out and resist rewetting. Thoroughly re-moisten by soaking the plant from the bottom.

you lack outdoor acreage, vermicomposting is a great way to create compost in a small space. This refers to using red worms to compost kitchen waste and make black, earthy-smelling, nutrient-rich humus perfect for use as a fertilizer and soil amendment. The worms actually do all of the work for you. You simply feed them table scraps and they produce castings (a delicate way of saying worm poop) that are rich in nutrients. Though it sounds like a messy proposition, worms can actually boast that their excretions don't stink! They will noiselessly convert mounds of otherwise smelly kitchen scraps such as coffee grounds, banana peels, and vegetable trimmings into a rich, nearly odorless soil amendment. If you are squeamish about worms, skip worm farming and buy already prepared worm castings. I buy worm castings, but not because I don't like worms. For over a year, I had a thriving worm bin, but then I got chickens. Soon, the chickens' appetite for table scraps outpaced the worms, and I eventually had no food for the worms, so I fed the worms to the chickens! Thank goodness commercial worm castings are now excellent and easy to obtain. However, if you don't have chickens or anything else vying for table scraps, worm composting is easier than you might think, and it can make an amusing and educational project for school-age children.

Organic fertilizers, instead of chemical ones, will also boost the humic content of your soils. Choose organic foods that say they are humus-based or contain humic acid, which is the byproduct of humus. Creating compost soup is another way to improve soil quality. This involves mixing ingredients such as compost and vermicompost in a barrel or bucket and steeping the contents over several days, which I discuss more thoroughly in chapter 4. This healthy, homemade soup is one of the best things you can feed your plants. It's rich in vitamins and nutrients and full of positive biological activity.

worms love my garbage

Worms are great allies in keeping soil alive; they aerate the soil and fertilize it with their excretions, known as castings. One way to bring their talents to your indoor garden is to start a worm farm in order to produce castings while disposing of your kitchen waste. Because a worm bin is virtually odorless and doesn't look like much more than a box filled with kitchen scraps and brown earth, it can be kept in the kitchen or nearby in a laundry room, utility room, or mud porch. If you prefer your worms further from your food preparation area, try keeping them in the garage, basement, or shed. They will survive temperatures as low as 50°F, but the most rapid feeding and compost making occurs from 55 to 77°F. Temperatures above 84°F can be harmful to the worms. Because I live in Southern California, I was able to keep my worm farm in my courtyard right outside my kitchen door. My worms thrived and produced plenty of worm castings for me—until the chickens, of course.

One word of caution about cats and worms. Keep the worm bin lid securely fastened, as felines love to use the worm bin as a litterbox. This won't hurt your cat, but it will harm the worms and may introduce parasites to the compost.

A worm farm can be started in just about any container, as long as it's shallow. A 2 × 2 foot box produces about 8 gallons of worm castings a month. To get your worm bin going, first make a bedding, which will hold moisture and provide a medium in which the worms can work. Bedding can consist of a combination of any of the following: shredded newspaper, shredded cardboard, leaf mold, peat moss, and compost. If you are making a 2 × 2 foot box, which is sufficient for the amount of food waste produced by two people, you will need four to six pounds of dry bedding.

A worm's body consists of 75 to 90% water, and the bedding should be 75% moisture. This can be obtained by weighing the bedding and adding three times as many gallons of water as dry bedding. The bedding usually soaks up the water. Once the bedding is prepared, add 1,000 red worms. Two good species are *Eisenia fetida* and *Lumbricus rubellus*. Red worms can be ordered through mail-order or found at bait shops or worm farms. They ship well and can be refrigerated for several days.

(continued)

A pound of worms will eat about a pound of garbage a day. When feeding your worms, keep in mind that they can more quickly break down soft, mushy foods. Chopping foods up and even grinding them in a food processor or blender is often a good idea as it speeds up the whole process. It's best not to add meat scraps, but worms do enjoy a wide variety of foods, including any type of produce, bread products, tea leaves, eggs and eggshells, coffee grounds, cakes/cookies, cereal, grits, cream of wheat, baked beans, oatmeal, and pancakes, to name a few leftovers.

Because worms breathe through their skin, which must be wet, keep the bin moist at all times by placing the worm farm in an area where it won't dry up or overheat. You can also contain moisture by placing a sheet of plastic on the top of the bedding and worms.

Bury the garbage in the bedding where the worms can more easily get to it. After a while, you will start to notice what your worms like best. When I had worms, I noted that they weren't particularly thrilled with tomatoes, but they really liked apple cores and cantaloupe rinds.

You only need a few simple ingredients to create a worm farm that will give you nutrient-rich vermicompost.

In about six weeks, you should begin to see changes in the bedding. It will get darker, and you'll notice a brown, earthlike material, which are the castings. You'll also see less bedding. This is the time to harvest your first batch of castings and to replace some of the bedding.

The best way to harvest castings is to simply dump out the contents of the bin on a piece of plastic and hand sort. If you're working indoors, you'll need a good lamp. Make several mounds of bedding and worms. With the light on, the worms will go to the bottom of each pile and bury themselves deep in the bedding. Scoop up the top of the bedding, which should contain a good amount of castings, and put it in a container. When you reach the worms at the bottom of each pile, return them and the remaining bedding to the compost bin. Then add new bedding and repeat the cycle.

Use the castings as a soil amendment and fertilizer in all of your potting soil. It can be added to already prepared mixes. Blend it in at a rate of 30% of soil volume. As mentioned in the mulch sidebar, it also makes an excellent mulch. Vermicompost not only conserves moisture and makes the soil biologically active, it also provides plants with a constant source of nutrients.

GOOD FUNGUS

Mention the word *fungus* to many gardeners, and they have visions of root rot. The truth is, some fungus is beneficial, such as mycorrhizal fungi, which form a symbiotic relationship with plants by attaching to their roots and bringing in more nutrients and water than a plant can on its own. Until now, mycorrhizal fungi have been recommended for outdoor growing, but recent research shows they definitely have a place in the indoor garden. As a matter of fact, many houseplants, with their tropical and subtropical backgrounds, survive in their native habitats because of mycorrhizal fungi. They depend on these fungi to provide them with water and nutrients.

Until recently, potting soil didn't include mycorrhizal fungi, which meant that care and feeding of houseplants could be considered an extreme sport! Today, if you begin to use one of the new potting soils that contain mycorrhizal fungi, your plants will have access to ample nutrients and be more drought tolerant. Mycorrhizal fungi are also sold separately in a dry form, which can be applied to the root zone.

These beneficial fungi are not a new discovery. For millions of years, mycorrhizal fungi have scavenged for nutrients and water in exchange for living on plant roots. Using the fungi indoors is a new phenomenon, though. Soil specialists have recently found that houseplants thrive when mycorrhizal fungi are added because they are able to scavenge all available water and nutrients from the restricted soil volume in a container, giving you a safety net when you forget to water or fertilize on a regular basis. Mycorrhizal fungi also help to unlock nutrients that are sometimes trapped in the soil. These fungi excrete enzymes that pull from the soil immobile nutrients like phosphorus and iron so that they become available to the plant. Using mycorrhizal fungi also makes plants stronger and disease resistant.

Many of the mycorrhizal products on the market contain fungus types that are well suited for indoor plants. In fact, orchids are the only category of houseplants for which there are no mycorrhizal fungi currently available commercially. Just about any houseplant will respond well to mycorrhizal fungi. With most houseplants, you're likely to see more vigorous growth, above and below ground, and more disease resistance. Within three weeks of using mycorrhizal fungi, many of my plants had better leaf color, more flowering and branching, and stronger overall health. Look at the root system and you'll also see many more feeder roots, which forage for water and nutrients.

To have luck with mycorrhizal products, it's important

we smell great—honest!

While humus, worm compost, and soil fungus might sound smelly, don't worry; they aren't. Humus generally has an earthy smell that you'd find with any potting soil, and worm compost usually has no odor. Mycorrhizal fungi are nearly microscopic and also odorless.

to use organic fertilizers because chemical fertilizers inhibit the fungus. When a plant has a diet of quickly absorbable fertilizer, it fails to activate the mycorrhizal fungi spores, which simply stay dormant. For best results, mycorrhizal fungi should be applied at the root zone of the plant, which you can do by either transplanting or making chambers in the soil with a pencil and putting the fungi in the holes. There are a variety of mycorrhizal species available commercially, and no one formula is better than another. Experiment with several to find out what works best for your indoor plant collection.

A WORD ABOUT SOIL pH

When a plant is ailing and produces stunted, weak growth despite proper care, the soil's pH may be the culprit. The degree of acidity or alkalinity is one of the last things gardeners check, but it should be one of the first. Many plant health problems are not caused by disease, insects, or nutritional deficiencies but rather by soil that is too acid or alkaline. Soil pH is vital to plant health. If it is too low or too high, many nutrients cannot be released to the plants.

A common example of this is phosphorus, which needs a pH near neutral to be available. Without this essential nutrient, plants can't perform various important functions, such as photosynthesis and root formation and growth.

You discover how important pH is when you grow citrus, ferns, gardenias, and other acid-loving plants, which share a common problem—chlorosis. Though this is actually due to iron deficiency in the plant, it's not always a lack of iron in the soil that leads to it. The soil may be too alkaline, and iron is best absorbed in acidic soils. For all plants, important nutrients such as calcium, magnesium, and nitrogen can also be tied up if pH isn't correct. Soil pH can also have an effect on the activity of soil microorganisms such as fungi and bacteria. A pH reading that is too high or low will lead to a loss of these microorganisms, which results in a less healthy soil overall. Burn is another by-product of a pH problem. While tip-burn might be construed as lack of water or overfertilizing, it may be a pH imbalance.

Soil pH is fairly easy to understand: It refers to a scale of acidity–alkalinity that ranges from 0 to 14, with the most common levels found between 4 and 8. Seven is neutral. Readings above 7 show alkalinity; readings below show acidity. While some houseplants such as ferns and philodendrons do well between 6 and 6.5—a little on the acidic side—other indoor plants like a more neutral to alkaline soil, such as dracaenas, palms, various Ficus, snake plant (*Sansevieria trifasciata*), and succulents. Each full point up or down the scale represents a tenfold increase or decrease in

checking your soil's pH

Test kits and meters are available for checking soil pH. Kits are sufficient if you have a small indoor garden and don't plan on testing very often. They range from $6 to $30, depending on the number of tests included and if they check for additional soil components, such as nitrogen.

A pH meter can be used indefinitely, requiring only occasional calibration. Accurate models generally cost $50 to $70—although I've had luck with less expensive meters. You can double-check the accuracy of your meter by also using soil test strips.

An easy-to-use pH meter gives you critical information about the soil your houseplants call home.

To test your soil pH, gather soil from a particular houseplant you'd like to test or take a collection from various pots to get an average reading. Air dry the soil before testing. Water is used in the testing process. You need water

(continued)

that is neutral pH, or your results will be skewed. Distilled water is a good choice, as it tends to be neutral. Some test kits come with water. To test, you simply mix soil with water. With kits, insert a test strip, remove it, and it will indicate a color. The strip is then compared to a chart that indicates pH levels. With a meter, you stick a prong into the soil and it automatically registers the pH level.

the degree of soil acidity and alkalinity. For example, a soil with a pH of 6 has 10 times more acid than one with a pH of 7, and soil with a pH of 5 is 100 times more acidic than the 7 soil. With this in mind, a full point change can mean the difference between life and death for certain plants. Most potting soils are neutral to start, but as they decompose, they become acidic over time. Alkaline water will raise pH, however, and fertilizer can also alter the reading. Once again, humus is your friend. It acts as a buffer and helps to stabilize soil pH at a desirable level.

To raise pH, amend with dolomite lime or oyster shell. To lower pH, amend with soil sulfur.

CHOOSING POTTING SOIL

Plant roots require several things of soil: moisture, air, and nutrients. The mixture you choose must offer all of these things. Most houseplants grow best in rich, well-drained soil with pumice or perlite as a draining agent. For plants that do best in always-moist conditions, choose soils that are heavy on vermiculite, peat moss, coconut coir, and even worm castings, or add more of these ingredients before planting.

All potting soils are somewhat different, so carefully check the soil's ingredients and consider your plant needs before purchasing. You'll want ample organic ingredients, such as various composts like vermicompost, bat and bird guano, feather meal, fish meal, alfalfa meal, bonemeal, and bloodmeal. Flowering plants generally do best in a mix containing organic water-holding materials such as shredded bark, compost, peat moss, and coconut coir. Such mixtures keep flowers and buds constantly moist and prevent bud drop. Some plants require their own special potting soil mix, such as African violets and other flowering plants, bromeliads, cacti, ferns, and epiphytes such as orchids.

If buying potting soil isn't your idea of real indoor gardening, you can blend your own. Most houseplants need good drainage yet ample air around their roots, so you will want to make a mix that contains some coarse, inorganic material (for drainage and aeration) and water-retaining organic materials. Horticultural sand is an inorganic material that facilitates drainage, while pumice and perlite aerate the soil and prevent compaction. Vermiculute holds water, making it especially good for moisture-loving plants. Good organic additions to a mix include compost like worm castings, aged manure (chicken and rabbit), fir bark, leaf mold, and peat moss.

HOMEMADE HUMUS-RICH MIX

This all-purpose potting soil mix is excellent for most houseplants. You can find all of the ingredients at the nursery, although some of the items may be found at home, such as the worm castings, if you have a worm farm, and compost, if you have a compost pile or bin. Never use beach sand, as this is extremely high in salt.

- 2 parts peat moss or coconut coir
- 3 parts compost
- 1 part horticultural sand
- 2 parts pumice or perlite
- 1 part vermicompost
- 1 tablespoon dolomite lime

While there are specialty soil mixes on the market, many aren't organic. Some even contain harsh synthetic fertilizers. Use the following soil blends if you are unable to find organic alternatives or if you simply want to mix your own. Doing so ensures that you know exactly what you're putting your houseplants in.

SPECIALTY SOIL MIXES

Blooming	2 parts peat moss or coconut coir, 1 part vermiculite, 1 part pumice or perlite, and 1 part vermicompost. Additional 2 tablespoons of bone meal or soft rock phosphate per gallon of soil.
Cactus/Succulent	2 parts compost or vermicompost, 1 part sand, and 2 parts perlite or pumice. Additional 2 tablespoons dolomite lime and ⅓ cup charcoal to each gallon of soil.
Orchids	Fir bark chips or pumice with 1 part vermicompost.
Citrus	2 parts peat moss or coconut coir, 1 part vermicompost, 1 part vermiculite, and 2 parts pumice or perlite. Additional 1 tablespoon of soil sulfur for each gallon of soil.
Ferns	2 parts peat moss or coconut coir, 1 part vermicompost, 2 parts pumice or perlite, 2 parts compost, and 1 part vermiculite.

3

wise watering

Can you guess the number one cause of houseplant death? Though pests and diseases seem likely culprits, most plants die because of improper watering. At first glance, watering seems like a no-brainer, but it's actually the indoor organic gardener's most challenging chore.

Water is necessary to plants for a number of reasons. Besides enabling them to stiffen and stand tall, it is essential to many chemical processes within the plant. Water is usually taken up from the soil through the roots, except in the case of epiphytes like orchids, which absorb water through their leaves. In the transpiration process, when moisture passes through plant breathing pores (stomata), plants release water into the atmosphere from their foliage. This has a suction effect that causes the plant to constantly pull water up through itself from the soil.

Damage from incorrect watering is common and runs the gamut from wilting and collapse to drowning.

Plants that survive despite watering mishaps often fail to thrive, resulting in a weak growth pattern, especially if the abuse continues. Even one missed watering can lead to poor growth for months afterward. And perhaps worst of all, many harmful pesticides are needlessly sprayed on plants that are infested with pests simply because of faulty watering.

ENOUGH ALREADY

Signs of overwatering include decayed leaves, brown and brittle leaf tips, scab-like bubbles on the underside of leaves, and something unexpected—wilting. Roots need to breathe but can't if they're in sopping soil with no air space. Continually wet soil leads to fungal disease in the roots, which shuts them down so they can't take up water and pass it on to the foliage. Many unknowing indoor gardeners make matters worse at this point by reacting to the wilted leaves and watering even more. Overwatering also leads to crown rot, which causes the crown to literally turn into mush.

HELP! I'M PARCHED!

Not watering a plant in time also causes wilting. While some plants spring back once they are watered and their leaves regain turgidity, others never completely recover. During drought, a plant will often let certain leaves or limbs die, leaving the plant unbalanced, sometimes permanently. Dieback usually corresponds to especially dry pockets in the soil. Other more tender plants will never really regain rigidity in their leaves. Drought some plants once, and you might as well throw them away. Thin-leaved plants are usually quicker to show underwatering symptoms. Plants with thick, succulent-like foliage tend to withstand dehydration better.

WATERING ON DEMAND

When it comes to watering, there are no hard and fast rules. I can only tell you to water plants when they need it. Some indoor gardeners wish to put their plants on a watering schedule. If you want to water every Tuesday, fine. Make that your day for checking all houseplants for water readiness and water only thirsty plants. Keep in mind that some plants may not cooperate and will want to be watered another day.

I've actually had heated discussions regarding watering schedules. Perhaps they're the same people who feel that babies should adapt to predetermined feeding times. I've seen gardens that are watered once a week whether they need it or not, and many of the plants are gasping for air. I'll be asked for tips on getting rid of pests and diseases or why certain plants can't seem to live. My answer is natural and simple—water only when the plants need it and watch them perk up and fight off troubles on their own.

When to water your plants will vary according to a variety of factors. Every home environment is different and plant watering needs differ by species. Determining when to water requires considering type of plant, time of year, ambient room temperature, light and humidity levels, soil density, and container type.

Type of Plant

Knowing each of your plant's watering requirements is your best line of defense. Research your plant (see this book's encyclopedia) and see how much water it needs. A variety of plants, such as African violets and citrus, like to be kept moist, while others, like cactus, prefer drying out between waterings. Some plants are especially particular about watering, and others are much more forgiving. Fast-growing plants and those that bloom or bear fruit require ample water. Underwater a flowering or fruiting plant in the bud stage, and it's likely to shed those future flowers and fruit. Plants with large leaves usually require more water than those with small leaves. And plants with leathery, waxy, or succulent leaves retain moisture and often require less water than plants with soft leaves.

Fortunately, most plants like to be watered when they're almost dry. Note that this doesn't mean bone dry—you don't want the roots to dry out, too. With an almost dry plant, the top inch or so is dry and the remainder of the soil will be dry very soon.

Pot-bound plants suffer from constant thirst because they have too many roots in a limited amount of soil. If your plant is a water hog, consider repotting and your watering chores will reduce substantially (see chapter 9).

Even when a plant is comfortable in its pot, the larger it grows, the more water it requires.

Time of Year

In general, spring and summer tend to be warmer and are active growth periods for many houseplants, so they'll be thirsty more often. Although many indoor plants require less water during the fall and winter months, forced air heating can dry out soil. Watch plants that are close to heating and air-conditioning vents. Hanging and elevated houseplants dry out the most quickly because warm air rises. Some plants retreat into a dormant state during winter and stop growing. Avoid root rot by never overwatering such plants.

Light, Temperature, and Humidity Levels

Plants in high light conditions will require more water than those in shadier spots. Plants located in a bright unobstructed eastern or western window generally dry out the fastest. Plants in high humidity draw moisture from the air and often need little watering. On the opposite end of the spectrum, plants in dry, low humidity environments may be often thirsty.

The temperature of your home also plays a part in how much water your plants consume. High temperatures mean high transpiration rates and thirsty plants. Outdoor temperature and weather conditions also affect your watering schedule. Dry, windy weather will have your plants calling for a drink. You can often put the watering can away in wet weather.

Soil Type

Heavy soil mixes that have a high percentage of peat moss and humus, such as compost, retain moisture longer than light mixes high in sand, perlite, or pumice. Determine the weight of a soil by picking up a small amount and squeezing it with your fingers after watering. If it forms a small ball, it is relatively heavy. If the ball falls apart easily, it is medium weight. The soil is light if you can't form a ball and it slips through your fingers.

Container Type

Many indoor gardeners are surprised to find that container choice plays a big part in how much or how little you must water. Terra-cotta pots are porous, which means these containers breathe and promote good air circulation. While this is ideal for some plants that require exceptional air circulation at the root zone, such as orchids, it also means that plants in clay pots must be watered more frequently. Avoid putting a water guzzler in such a pot.

Plastic pots are nonporous and the soil dries from the top down, which means they stay moist much longer. Watering chores are less with such pots, but overwatering becomes more likely. Glazed pots are also nonporous. Keep in mind that smaller containers dry out more readily than larger ones.

CHECKING FOR WATER READINESS

Watering your plants when the potting mix looks dry may seem like a good idea, but it's not always your best bet. Here are some reliable methods of checking to see if your plant needs watering.

The Finger Test

Nothing is quite as portable and readily accessible as your finger. Stick your forefinger in the soil up to your first knuckle. If the soil is dry, water. This method is best used for plants in medium-sized pots. Sticking your finger in small pots can disturb roots and large pots are often too deep.

For a modified version of the finger test that works in large pots, try the chopstick test. Stick a wooden chopstick deep into the soil and remove. If the chopstick is damp and soil is sticking to it, no water is required. When it comes out clean and dry, it's time to water.

Moisture meters quickly indicate when a plant needs a drink.

using a moisture meter

For a more scientific method, especially preferred for determining the water readiness of large plants, try a moisture meter. Stick this pronged instrument into the soil, and a gauge will indicate when a plant needs watering. Such instruments operate with an electrical current. The strength of the current depends on the relative amount of moisture in the soil. Be aware that it is possible to get inaccurate readings. This occurs when the meter has worn out or when the potting soil is high in accumulated salts. In the latter case, consider repotting (see chapter 9). Always check several areas of a pot and double-check with another method when a reading seems questionable.

Tools such as moisture meters enable you to pinpoint exactly when a plant requires watering.

The Pick-Up Test

This method works well with small- to medium-sized containers. Simply lift the container. Dry soil weighs considerably less than wet soil, so a lightweight container often means a plant is thirsty. One clever indoor gardener I know of keeps her houseplant on a postage meter. She waters when it becomes less weighty.

The Eye Test

Pay close attention, and you'll soon recognize the signals each of your plants give when watering is required. Hydrated plants look right. Their cells are turgid with water and they stand firm. Many plants flag when they're thirsty, getting a dull sheen to their leaves and appearing slightly limp. Catching a plant at this point, before it actually wilts, can save it from permanent underwatering damage.

When you're new to watering your houseplants or when you're unsure, use more than one method.

HOW TO WATER

Water in the morning, if possible. If you can only water your plants at midnight, however, do so rather than droughting them. I confess to sometimes watering my plants in the wee hours. Mornings are rushed for me. Nights are often quiet and give me a chance to examine my plants and see who needs a good drink. If you water at night, be careful not to get water at the crown of the plant or on the leaves. Water sitting on plants overnight can lead to fungal disease.

Always water with tepid to warm water—never cold. Cold water has been shown to send houseplants into shock and can cause dark spots on the foliage. I use water that is a little warmer than room temperature.

Most plants do best if watered from above. When possible, bring the plant to the sink and let the water slowly run through the pot until the container is heavy with moisture. If a plant's soil is overly dry, this may mean running water through it at a slow pace several times until the soil becomes saturated. I've found that slightly squeezing plastic pots as you water them helps to resaturate the soil more quickly.

Watering well by flooding your houseplants is important for a number of reasons. First, the water percolating down through the soil adds oxygen. Flooding also helps ensure good root development. If all you ever do is sprinkle the top half of the soil with water, the plant won't form roots in the lower half.

Flooding also leaches harmful salts out of the soil, preventing salt buildup that will occur over time. This buildup readily shows up on terra-cotta pots as white rings. On plastic pots, salt rings appear at the top of the pot and around the drainage holes and as a yellow or white crust on the soil surface. Soluble salts damage plant roots and hinder water uptake. Signs of salt stress include reduced growth, brown leaf tips, dropping of lower leaves, small new growth, dead root tips, and wilting associated with root rot. Weakened plants are also susceptible to attack from insects and diseases.

Watering large plants at the kitchen sink is often impractical. Using a thin-spouted watering can, water on location until water comes out of the drainage holes. Your large plants should be in waterproof cachepots or on drip trays that have one to two inches of marbles, pebbles, or a similar material (see chapter 6). This system allows excess water to rinse through and away from the bottom of the pot and humidifies surrounding air. Avoid letting the bottom of the pot sit in water, as it will reabsorb salt that you just washed away and it can lead to fungal problems associated with root rot. Use a turkey baster or an old sponge to remove any excess.

when leaching is good

The best way to prevent salt build-up is to leach your plants, which refers to rinsing the soil. The water used to leach a pot should equal at least twice the volume of the pot. If a layer of salt has formed on the crust of the soil, remove before leaching. When the soluble salt level is particularly high, it's often best to repot (see chapter 9). Or try using a salt leaching solution in the water. These contain free-floating chelates that capture the salts as you water the plant and flush it out of the soil. Leach every three to four months for best results.

Avoid pots without drainage holes. Use them as cachepots, instead.

For elevated out-of-the-way plants, consider investing in a hose designed specifically for indoor watering. Such hoses are used with a watering wand and can be attached to the faucet. Many stretch a good distance, allowing you to water out-of-reach plants more easily. For such a watering method, you would obviously need a good drainage situation. Keep in mind that many hanging planters have flimsy, useless drip trays that are only as wide as the pot. A better solution is using a metal carrying-basket into which you can place a pot and drip tray or cachepot.

NO DOUSING, PLEASE

Some plants are an exception to the top-watering rule. African violets and other fuzzy-leaved plants are prone to water spots and fungal disease and are better watered from the bottom, especially in humid climates. Bottom water-

Some plants, such as African violets, prefer bottom watering.

ing is also the only way to rehydrate plants that have become very dry. In such cases soil shrinks away from the sides of the pot and repels rather than retains water.

To bottom water, set the pot in a container of water that is slightly bigger in size. Capillary action—the movement of water from the wettest part of the potting mix to the driest—will draw water into the soil. Soak until bubbles stop coming to the surface and the plant is saturated. If the plant is so dry that it's having difficulty drinking, add a slight amount of water from above, which will often start the cycle in motion.

HOW'S YOUR WATER?

The water you pour on houseplants should be pure and clear of any contaminants. Avoid artificially softened water, as this is toxic to plants. Some indoor gardeners question the wisdom of using tap water. In many cases, it's fine. If there are any problems with tap water, it's usually an

automatic watering

If your time is limited or you vacation frequently, consider more automated watering methods. Wick irrigation involves a wick that sits in a water reservoir down below the plant and is threaded up through the bottom of the pot; this is best used for plants that require constant, even moisture, such as African violets and ferns. The wick continually draws on the water reservoir, transporting just the right amount of water to the plant. A wick system can be found at various nurseries and mail-order plant suppliers, or you can make your own. When doing so, use a synthetic wick material such as acrylic yarn. Cotton or wool do not work well. Keep the reservoir full, and periodically check the soil to ensure that the wick system is working.

A similar invention are self-watering pots. These are usually constructed of plastic and have a water reservoir and a device that taps the stored water when the potting soil dries out.

elevation in chlorine or fluoride or excess mineral salts. Salts can cause root tips to burn and eventually die back and high fluoride content leads to tip burn. If certain plants exhibit sensitivity issues, try another kind of water such as reverse osmosis—processed water, distilled water, or rainwater. Periodic leaching and repotting also helps.

GO SOILLESS

There are those indoor gardeners who choose to skip soil and grow in water. Known as hydroponics, growing plants without soil is popular with sensitive individuals who have allergies and auto-immune issues. Cultivating houseplants in water and a soilless medium such as rock wool, coconut coir, or expanded clay also allows plants to grow bigger

In areas where pollution isn't excessive, rainwater is an excellent source of water for your plants. Catch it and bring it indoors, or put houseplants outdoors in gentle showers. A good soak from the sky allows plants to draw fresh water through their roots while washing away excessive salt and fertilizer build-up. When there is thunder and lightning, rain also delivers a dilute form of nitric acid, which will make your plants even happier. And rainwater is acidic, which some indoor plants like.

Growing plants (such as bulbs) hydroponically creates an interesting indoor garden display.

faster. All nutrition is supplied through the water, so plants can put energy into foliage rather than root growth.

Because hydroponically grown plants are completely dependent on water for their nutrition, it's important to use an organic liquid fertilizer that has macro- and micronutrients. Look for fertilizers that are labeled for hydroponics. Compost tea that has been strained is also an excellent food (see chapter 4).

Change the water solution every two weeks and check the pH on a regular basis. It should generally fall in the 6.0–6.5 range. There are products to lower or raise pH as needed.

4

feed your foliage friends a gourmet organic feast

The fast food epidemic harming our society is also hurting our indoor gardens. Countless well meaning houseplant growers routinely overfeed their plants with quick-acting synthetic fertilizers that promise "miraculous" results. Such foods do promote rapid foliage growth, but at the expense of the plant's life force—its root system. By mainlining your plants with chemical food, you skip the critical step of feeding the soil that roots call home. Artificial fertilizers sterilize potting medium by killing beneficial soil microbes and fungi. A lifeless soil is unable to feed the plant, making your foliage friend completely dependent on you for sustenance. Abruptly stop feeding an "addicted" plant and you put it under extreme stress. Synthetic fertilizers can also alter the soil pH and create toxic-salt syndrome. And an unbalanced plant with more foliage than roots is a target for pests and diseases.

If you take a natural approach and feed your soil with organic fertilizers, you indirectly nourish your plants. When you nurture the soil and the organisms in it, you give your plants a balanced diet that allows things to work as nature intended. Organics provide your houseplants and the soil with a slow-release, consistent nourishment. Such a health food diet makes your foliage friends strong and self-sustaining. Rather than depend on you for their every morsel, they'll find what they need in the soil. As in nature, an organic soil alive with microbes and fungi makes nutrients slowly available to plants. By enriching their soil with organic supplements and encouraging the growth of naturally occurring beneficial organisms, you give your plants the tools they need to access nutrients in the soil and the strength to protect themselves against harmful pathogens and pests. The houseplant in organic soil is like a well-trained athlete—efficiently burning its fuel and staying at the top of its game.

JUST A LITTLE FOOD

If you're suspecting that organically fed houseplants need less food than those on a fast food diet, you're right. Some of my own plants go for months without a feeding because their soil sustains them. Fertilizing is still important, however. Well-fed plants lead to happier greenery with lusher, quicker growth. Flowering plants also require fertilizer to bloom.

Signs that your houseplants need feeding include yellowing leaves, less new growth, and smaller growth when you get it. Failure to flower is another sign.

Note that yellowing leaves are also a sign of too much watering. If you're watering correctly, however, (see chapter 3), then you probably have a nitrogen or mineral deficiency.

WHAT DO ALL THOSE NUMBERS MEAN?

The set of three hyphenated numbers on a fertilizer bottle signifies the analysis of the food. These numbers stand for the nitrogen, phosphorus, and potassium content of the fertilizer. Commonly referred to as N-P-K, these nutrients are found in complete organic fertilizers and are critical to plant growth.

N-P-K

Nitrogen   Phosphorus   Potassium

The set of three hyphenated numbers on fertilizers signifies the nitrogen, phosphorus, and potassium content of the food, which are the three major nutrients that plants require.

Nitrogen is key in the production of chlorophyll. This major nutrient stimulates leaf growth and keeps foliage green. A lack of nitrogen is the most common nutrient deficiency. It stunts a plant and causes leaves to yellow. Older foliage turns completely yellow, dries, and falls off. On the other hand, too much nitrogen produces overly abundant new, soft growth susceptible to insect infestation.

Phosphorus is responsible for promoting sturdy cell structure, healthy root growth, and abundant flower and fruit production. Without sufficient phosphorus, many flowering plants simply won't bloom and plants will lose their overall vigor.

Potassium is an all-encompassing nutrient that plays an important role in photosynthesis and water and nutrient management. It also strengthens plants against pests and diseases. Potassium deficiencies often show up on the margins of large-leafed plants. The margins of older leaves become brown, dry, and brittle.

The Minor League

For healthy growth, plants also need small amounts of other nutrients, which are often called micronutrients. Many, such as calcium and magnesium, work in tandem to give houseplants what they need. If houseplant soil lacks any of the minor players, you'll see a variety of deficiencies, especially in mature plants.

Magnesium is essential in the formation of chlorophyll and with its partner, calcium, plays a fundamental role in the manufacture of cells and their growth. A fairly common deficiency, insufficient calcium and magnesium lead to distorted new growth that doesn't develop completely, as well as yellow dotting near the newest growth.

Sulfur is another essential micronutrient. It acts with nitrogen in making protoplasm for new plant cells and brings out the fragrance in aromatic plants.

Iron and zinc work together for cellular reproduction. Deficiencies in this duo lead to yellow dotting that starts midway into the plant and heads for new growth. And iron and zinc deficiency in some plants, such as citrus plants, leads to chlorosis. Most products that treat iron deficiency have chelated iron because iron alone cannot be absorbed by plants. It must be paired with zinc to be effective.

CHOOSING ORGANIC FOODS

Thanks to the widespread movement toward gardening organically outdoors, there are now a multitude of organic fertilizers on the market, from complete foods with macro- and micronutrients to supplements that contain a single nutrient.

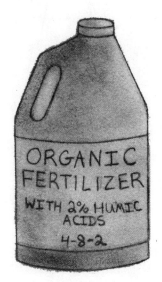

Fortunately, it's fairly easy to spot organic fertilizer. Just look for a low N-P-K ratio. Those foods that have numbers 10 and under are often organic. Something like a 20-20-20 is generally a synthetic mix and should be avoided. I know choosing foods with less nutrients goes against

Organic fertilizers generally have a low N–P–K ratio. Good foods also contain humic acids, as well as micronutrients.

the grain for some of you. Just remember that in this case, more is not better. Mixes with a high concentration of synthetic nutrients simply bombard a plant, destroying precious soil microbes and fungi. Ironically, plants absorb very little nutrition from such high-powered foods. Most simply washes through the plant.

organic fertilizers

The foods in this list feed plants as well as the soil.

- Alfalfa meal [Natural growth stimulant; plus trace minerals]
- Bat and bird guano [Nitrogen and calcium]
- Bloodmeal [Nitrogen]
- Bonemeal (liquid) [Phosphorus, calcium, and trace minerals]
- Chicken manure [Nitrogen]
- Cottonseed meal [Nitrogen; phosphorus; potassium; also acidifies soil]
- Epsom salts [Magnesium]
- Feather meal [Nitrogen]
- Fish emulsion (some new products smell like the ocean rather than dead fish) [Nitrogen, phosphorus, potassium, and trace minerals]
- Fish meal [Nitrogen, phosphorus, and potassium]
- Greensand [Calcium, iron, magnesium, potassium, and trace minerals]
- Humic acids [Organic matter and trace minerals]
- Kelp meal [Potassium and trace minerals]
- Oyster shells [Calcium]
- Seaweed (liquid) [Trace minerals and natural growth hormones]
- Soft Rock Phosphate [Phosphorus and calcium]
- Worm castings / Vermicompost [Trace minerals]

Good organic fertilizers are products of natural decomposition and are easy for plants to digest. They are derived from simple sources that come from the earth and you should recognize them and their ingredients. Carefully read the labels on your fertilizer bottles or bags as closely as you inspect the ingredient lists on foods. Choose products with nutrients in their elemental form (remember the periodic table of elements you learned in high school). Avoid products that have been engineered or altered. For instance, super triple phosphate is a harsh manmade form of phosphorus.

Also check to see that your all-purpose food has micronutrients such as magnesium, iron, and zinc. When a food is lacking in certain nutrients, supplementing is necessary. If your fertilizer does not contain magnesium, add a pinch of Epsom salts (magnesium sulfate). Liquid seaweed is a great overall supplement that will provide trace elements. And I always recommend adding humic acid, which is critical to soil health (see chapter 2) and improves nutrient uptake and management. There are a few fertilizers containing humic acids (Gro-Power is one), or you can buy humic acid separately. You can also add humic acid and other minor elements to your plants with a compost tea, which is mild enough that it can be used at any time and in conjunction with other fertilizers (see recipe below).

Various organic root biostimulants are another good addition to your feeding regimen. These relatively new introductions to the organic gardening scene generally contain a combination of seaweed, humic acids, and vitamin B1—all great ingredients for promoting soil fertility, root development, and healthy, vibrant foliage.

LIQUID VERSUS GRANULAR?

I suggest using liquid fertilizer indoors. It's easy—you simply mix and water. Because they've gone through a decomposition process during their manufacture, they tend to smell very little, if at all. You can also tinker with their strength until you come up with a solution you like.

The only time I use granular food is when I repot. I mix it into the potting soil at half strength. I'm not a big fan of adding dry food to established pots because you disturb roots, it's easier for salts to collect on the top of your soil, and the food sometimes grows mold.

In general, stay away from plant spikes. They usually contain high amounts of chemical fertilizer and are notorious for causing toxic salt build-up.

FOLIAR FEEDING

Besides delivering food to your plants through the soil and their roots, you can also apply it directly to their leaves, where plants will quickly take up nutrients. While some experts push foliar feeding as a plant's main source of nourishment because it's so easy to metabolize, I don't recommend using it on a regular basis. One of the major reasons is that it doesn't feed the soil. Foliar feeding is most effectively used to address a deficiency that needs immediate attention. It's an excellent idea when there are signs of specific micronutrient deficiencies. For instance, chlorosis on citrus calls for a spray of iron chelate. Always use an organic food marked for foliar feeding, and test a leaf an hour or two before treatment to make sure that no damage occurs. If you spray compost tea—which can boost the spirits of an ailing plant—strain it before using, as any particles left on foliage can attract bacteria.

a better brew: making compost tea

We all know that compost is the ultimate ingredient of an organic garden. While you can and should apply it to your homemade potting mixes and use it as a topdressing, I've also found that making compost tea is an excellent addition to your organic food arsenal. You can use regular compost or vermicompost. Mix a gallon of compost with three gallons of water and let it sit overnight. Scoop out the brown tea that forms on top and use it on your plants. If you'll be using it as a foliar fertilizer, it's important to strain it.

Foliar feeding also helps to acclimate new plants (see chapter 1). A good spray of seaweed, which contains a natural hormone, does wonders for shell-shocked plants.

FEEDING YOUR HOUSEPLANTS

Many books advise feeding with every watering, but that's for indoor gardens on chemical diets. Houseplants grown organically don't need to eat that often. As a matter of fact, less is better when it comes to houseplant food. When you do fertilize, dilute the food to one-half to one-quarter strength.

Feeding should be associated with the growth of the plant and the time of year. It's best to skip feedings altogether in the middle of winter, when a plant appears to have stopped growing. Also keep in mind that the longer you treat your soil organically, the higher the fertility of the soil and the less fertilizer a plant will need.

I suggest doing a regular maintenance feeding four to six

fertilizer burn

When plants get too much food, they exhibit symptoms of marginal burn. In this case, the whole margin of a leaf turns brown, as opposed to the leaf tip. In severe cases, the leaves will actually curl under. When you suspect a toxicity, leach the root zone well (see chapter 3). Flushing should be done as a preventative measure every three to four months.

times a year, with extra feedings and special supplements as your plants require it. Bloomers that are just budding up have a high metabolism and will need extra phosphorus-rich food, while foliar plants beginning growth in the spring require a good dose of nitrogen. Plants in strong light usually need more food than those in darker locations. It will vary from plant to plant and situation to situation.

Avoid fertilizing sick or weak plants because it will overtax their systems. Remember that fertilizer is more like a vitamin—not a medicine. Instead, fix the cultural problems like poor lighting that lead to the problem in the first place, and resume fertilizing when the plant is well.

Always moisten plant soil before applying fertilizer—even liquid varieties. This is particularly important for plants with sensitive roots, like ferns and orchids. To prevent salt build-up in the soil, remove excess fertilizer water from the humidity tray or cachepot.

5

shedding light

Nurseries might go out of business if indoor gardeners only knew how important proper lighting is to house-plants. Unlike humans and animals, plants produce most of their own food. Light triggers and energizes the process of photosynthesis. This procedure makes the carbohy-drates that fuel plants. You can use the best organic gar-dening practices, but without sufficient light, plants can't photosynthesize and instead use stored food to maintain growth. As the plant wears down its energy reserves, it can-nibalizes itself, eventually starving to death. This explains why a plant may seem to be doing well in a poor lighting situation for a time and then fail.

While some plants die when lighting is poor, others get just enough light to live a feeble existence. Plants receiving insufficient light display poor growth, have sparse foliage, refuse to flower, and are more prone to pests and diseases.

Both light intensity (the amount available) and duration (length of exposure) are important to plant health. Give your indoor garden the right mixture of both and you'll have few problems.

LIGHT INTENSITY

The strength of light available to plants is important, as some plants require more light than others. Light intensity is affected by a variety of factors, some of which you can control. Clean windows let in more light than dirty ones. Heavy curtains create a lot of shade, but sheers or blinds brighten a space. The size and type of window also affects intensity. The larger the windows, the more luminous the interior. Bay windows that extend out beyond the building create more light than flush ones. Skylights brighten otherwise dim interiors. Exterior obstructions such as plants, roof overhangs, and surrounding buildings also affect how powerful lighting is. Inside the home, pale-colored and white walls and mirrors tend to reflect light and make a space lighter, while dark-colored walls absorb light and darken a room. How far a plant is from a window also determines how much light is received. Light concentration diminishes the further you move away.

WHAT'S YOUR ORIENTATION?

A big factor in light intensity is orientation, which refers to the direction a window faces. In the Northern Hemisphere,

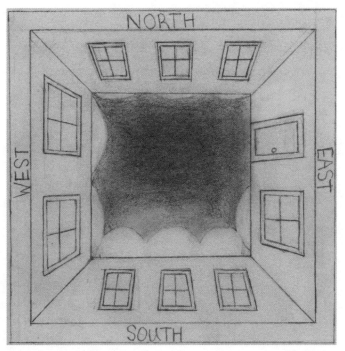

Some windows will provide your houseplants more light than others depending on the orientation of your home.

southern windows are often ideal for growing houseplants, as they let in bright light throughout the day. (It is the opposite in the Southern Hemisphere.) Sun-loving plants thrive in a southern window, and plants that like medium light do well when placed away from such windows. This orientation is especially helpful in the winter months, when other windows receive much less light. Watch for leaf scorching in the summer, however, because such windows can get intense heat. Move plants back when necessary.

Eastern windows are another good spot for many houseplants. They let in full sun for a short period in the morning and medium light all day. Morning sun is mild and rarely burns foliage. Light drops off rapidly as you move away from an east-facing window.

Western exposure windows receive bright light all day long and direct sun in the afternoon. Plants in such windows do best when protected from the intense afternoon sun by blinds, sheer curtains, or on the exterior by a roof overhang, awning, or neighboring trees or buildings. Light levels drop off quickly as you move away from these windows.

North-facing windows are often considered the least desirable because they offer little light. They are, however, a good location for certain plants like African violets, and the light level is usually of medium strength when plants are placed right in front of the window. (In the Southern Hemisphere, a northern exposure is like our southern exposure and the most desirable location for growing plants.)

When assessing light levels in a room, keep in mind adjacent windows. I grow a wide variety of plants in my dining room, which has windows on the north and west walls, giving it a low to medium light intensity. African violets thrive along the northern windows.

Of course, every house is different. In order to give each plant the right amount of light, it's important to observe your home's lighting throughout the day and seasons.

LIGHT DURATION

The length of time light enters windows varies by season. Plants get less light overall during short winter days. As the angle of the sun's rays moves throughout the year, how light hits your windows also changes. This is especially true of south-facing windows. More light actually enters these locations during cooler months because the angle of the sun's rays is lowest. In winter, south-facing windows are often a good location for high light lovers that usually grow in eastern or western windows.

MEASURING LIGHT

Knowing the orientation of your windows helps determine available light, but to accurately measure the quantity of light in each room, I suggest using a light meter. I resisted using one for years, and I got along fairly well without it. However, once I tried a light meter and discovered how far off I was in my estimations, I realized how handy

Light meters are a useful tool for measuring the light available to your houseplants.

this little tool can be. Knowing the exact amount of light a room gets helps you make the right decisions in plant placement. Some indoor gardeners use a photographer's light meter, but they are designed to be sensitive to the same light wavelengths as the human eye, which is not what a plant sees. It's best to use a plant light intensity meter. Such gadgets measure the wavelengths used for photosynthesis and chlorophyll production.

Light meters usually show foot-candles, which is the amount of light a candle gives off in all directions one foot from the flame. The light intensity of a sunny summer day is approximately 10,000 foot-candles. Some meters show low, medium, or high, while others show foot-candle measurements. Each meter measures slightly differently, and some are more accurate than others. A little knowledge is always helpful, though, and if nothing else, a meter can confirm what you think about a certain lighting situation.

Tips to keep in mind when using a light meter:

1. Measure the light intensity at leaf level.
2. Consult a table of light requirements (see sidebar below).
3. Take readings at different times of the day from various locations near the plant and at several distances from the light source.

Though it's not as accurate or complete, you can also use the shadow test, which refers to the amount of shadow cast by your hand onto a white piece of paper. A barely visible shadow indicates low light, a more discernable shadow medium light, and a sharp, high-contrast shadow shows high light conditions.

Plants with low and medium light requirements generally grow well in most homes that have windows facing in several directions. Plants with high light requirements only do well in sunny windows or with supplemental lighting.

If you wish to place a certain plant in a location that doesn't offer enough light, give it an energizing dose of light several times a week by moving it to a sunny window for the day.

TOO MUCH OR NOT ENOUGH?

Signs of inadequate light:

- Stretching and reaching for light.
- Sparse growth, with long distances between leaf sets (dense growth indicates adequate light).
- Lower foliage loss (available light can only sustain top leaves).
- Overall loss of vitality. Leaves may be pale and flowers may be nonexistent.
- Pest and disease problems.

Though more uncommon, an excessive amount of light will scorch leaves. Burning usually occurs in south- or west-facing windows that heat up at certain times of the year.

light candle levels

Some of the plants listed can also be grown in higher light. The categories in which they appear indicate the lowest light possible for them to thrive.

Low-light Plants (50 to 100 foot-candles):

Arrowhead vine (*Syngonium podophyllum*)

Cast-iron plant (*Aspidistra elatior*)

Chinese evergreen (*Aglaonema modestum*)

Dracaenas, various

Peace lily (*Spathiphyllum wallisii*)

Pothos (*Epipremnum aureum*)

Philodendron (*P. scandens*)

Radiator plant (*Peperomia species*)

Snake plant (*Sansevieria trifasciata*)

Medium-light Plants (100 to 300 foot-candles):

African violet (*Saintpaulia species*)

Aluminum plant (*Pilea species*)

Anthurium species and hybrids

Coleus × hybridus

Ctenanthe species

Creeping fig (*Ficus pumila*)

Croton (*Codiaeum species*)

Dracaenas, various

Dumb Cane (*Dieffenbachia* hybrids)

Ferns, various

Fiddle-leaf fig (*Ficus lyrata*)

Firecracker flower (*Crossandra infundibuliformis*)

Gloxinia (*Sinningia speciosa*)

Goldfish plant (*Columnea* species)

Grape ivy (*Cissus rhombifolia*)

Lipstick plant (*Aeschynanthus species*)

Nerve plant (*Fittonia* verschaffeltii)

Palms, various

Peacock plant (*Calathea zebrina*)

Polka-dot plant (*Hypoestes phyllostachya*)

Prayer plant (*Maranta leuconeura*)

Purple velvet plant (*Gynura species*)

Rubber tree (*Ficus elastica*)

Schefflera species

Spider plant (*Chlorophytum comosum*)

Split-leaf philodendron (*Monstera deliciosa*)

Wandering Jew (*Tradescantia zebrina/Zebrina pendula*)

High-light Plants (300+ foot-candles):

Begonia

Bloodleaf (*Iresine*)

Cacti/Succulents

Citrus, various

Ficus benjamina

Orchids, various

Wax plant (*Hoya carnosa*)

Zebra plant (*Aphelandra squarrosa*)

Signs of too much light:

- Scorched leaves that are browned or bleached on the window side.
- Overall yellowing and thickening of new growth.
- Excessively compact and stunted growth.
- Foliage curled downward.
- Wilting when adequate moisture is present in the soil.
- Lighter than normal leaves.

Rectify overlighting conditions by moving plants away from the window or installing adjustable shades, curtains, or blinds.

ARTIFICIAL LIGHTING

Supplemental lighting is one of the few artificial items I suggest you use when growing houseplants organically. While sunshine is ideal for houseplants because it provides the full spectrum of color that plants require for growth, it's not always available or sufficient. Whether your home is dark or you would like to supplement your

Some plants thrive under artificial lighting, such as flowering plants like gloxinia.

existing light, today's wide variety of lighting products make it possible and fairly simple to do.

While this can get very technical, there are three main types of artificial lighting—fluorescent, full-spectrum, and HID.

Fluorescent Lighting

Your most inexpensive option is fluorescent lighting. Use a combination of one cool and one warm bulb. Warm-white tubes have an enhanced red range, which plants need for flowering and overall development, and cool whites have an enhanced blue range, which promotes compact growth. Fluorescent lights come in tubes and bulbs, which can be installed into regular lamps and shop lights. They're relatively cool and won't burn plants like incandescent bulbs.

Fluorescents work well for low-growing plants that require low to medium light. The closer to the bulb the plants are, the more light they'll receive. For maximum light, the top of the plant should be 3 to 12 inches from the bulb. Fluorescents should be changed every year, regardless of how they appear, as they tend to break down.

Full-Spectrum Lighting

A similar, increasingly popular option is the use of full-spectrum lights, which also come in tubes and individual light bulbs. These simulate the sun at noon and provide clear, brilliant light that can do wonders for an indoor garden. Currently a favorite option in offices, full-spectrum lights shower a space with natural light, reducing eye strain and boosting productivity. They are also cool, emitting no adverse heat.

Be cautious about what type of lights you buy, as some marketed as "gro-bulbs" are full spectrum, while others are little more than colored incandescent bulbs.

High Intensity Light Systems (HID)

Long used by commercial greenhouses, HID lighting not only duplicates but also magnifies what the sun can do. With this powerful lighting, gardeners can grow just about anything indoors, including tropical plants like bananas and high light lovers like tomatoes. While the average indoor gardener generally doesn't require a HID system, it is the best option for high light plants that flower and fruit and for spaces that have very little natural light. These generally costly fixtures can be found through mail-order and specialty lighting suppliers. They require special wiring and a ballast box, which boosts the supply of power going to them. There are two main types. Metal halide lamps emit strong light at the blue end of the spectrum, which encourages leaf growth, especially in young plants, while high pressure sodium lights give off red wavelengths, which boosts flowering. Commercial greenhouses tend to use both types of light, depending on the stage of growth. High intensity lights are usually very hot, so plants should be placed 10 to 12 feet away.

HOW LONG?

In general, if you are supplementing existing light, you should set a timer for an extra 4 to 8 hours of light before sunrise or after sunset. When the light is your only source, run for 8 to 12 hours a day. Plants like regularity in their lighting schedule, so use a timer.

take a turn for the better

Natural light from windows comes in at a slant, not from above like outdoors, so plants tend to lean toward the light. You can encourage your plants to stand tall by giving them a quarter turn in the same direction once or twice a month.

EXPERIMENT

It's hard to know which plants will do well under lights and how close they should be placed. Make adjustments until a plant does well.

Some plants that take readily to artificial lighting include African violets, most gesneriads, miniature geraniums, gloxinia, orchids, ferns, and even azaleas, bougainvillea, and citrus.

6

it's a jungle in here . . . or at least it should be: providing your houseplants with humidity

Do you have houseplants that seem to curl up and wither away or have problems with brown leaf tips? If your indoor garden is ailing despite your best efforts, suspect an inappropriate humidity level.

When it comes to growing healthy, happy houseplants, one of the most overlooked aspects of plant care is humidity. Most houseplants originally come from the floors of tropical jungles where the air is so heavy with humidity that a jungle dweller's clothes remain perpetually wet. Not exactly a replica of most homes. Our living environments may seem comfortable to us, but they resemble the Sahara Desert to sensitive plants. Although many of these tropical descendants will survive in our parched indoor air, most do much better with a little extra moisture.

A few finicky members of the houseplant family require additional humidity to survive, such as *Anthurium*, orchids, African violets, ferns, and zebra plant (*Aphelandra squarrosa*).

Plants quickly protest low atmospheric humidity. At first, the leaves will yellow or the leaf edges or tips will brown. Leaf curling, starting at the bottom and making its way to the top, is another sign. Leaves actually twist up and fall off and flower buds shrivel and drop. If the plant loses a large amount of leaves, it can't manufacture food and will eventually collapse. Worse still, in such a weakened state, plants are unable to resist disease and infection. This leads to many indoor gardeners spraying potent harmful pesticides, poisoning their homes and themselves. Providing plants with humidity helps keep them healthy and your indoor garden organic.

Whereas we perspire, plants transpire. The process is somewhat different, but the principle is the same. Water evaporates from our skin when we perspire in order to stabilize our body temperature. Plants transpire in an attempt to add moisture to their environment, losing water to the air through their stomata (breathing pores). They transpire heaviest in dry air. If we spend any length of time in low humidity, our eyes, nose, and throat membranes become irritated. If a plant spends any length of time in low moisture, it suffers damage.

WHAT IS HUMIDITY?

Humidity is water suspended in the air as a vapor. It is the amount of actual moisture per cubic foot of air. The term "relative humidity" refers to the percentage of moisture in the air sampled at a specific location, taking into consideration the total amount of moisture that particular air can hold without the vapor being precipitated into rain or fog. A reading of 50% humidity indicates that the air sample contains half of the moisture it can hold before the moisture condenses and becomes visible.

The amount of water that the air is capable of holding is not constant. It is directly related to air temperature. The warmer the temperature, the more moisture the air can hold. Warm air can sustain greater amounts of humidity without precipitating. A temperature of 75°F matched with 50% humidity—an ideal scenario for houseplants—carries more humidity than a temperature of 52°F and 50% humidity. Morning dew is caused by falling night temperatures. As the air cools, it is capable of holding less and less moisture. The excess precipitates out and falls to the ground.

HOW MUCH HUMIDITY?

In general, houseplants require at least 40 to 60% humidity. The humidity of your home depends on a variety of factors, such as where you live and current weather conditions. Indoor air quality in Arizona, for instance, is going to be much drier than in a home in South Carolina. Moist rainy days will provide more humidity than dry parching ones. In Southern California, we have strong,

measuring humidity

You can test the humidity level of your home with a hygrometer (also called a humidistat or humidity meter). This instrument measures moisture in the air and can be found at some nurseries, hardware stores, and via mail-order.

Hygrometers measure both humidity and temperature to give you an idea of the relative humidity. Older types of hygrometers were mechanical and rudimentary, but newer ones are digital and run on batteries. They don't need to be independently calibrated and usually function with an error of 1 to 3%, depending on product quality. There are models that illuminate in the dark or that can be attached to walls or cabinets. Digital hygrometers are portable and

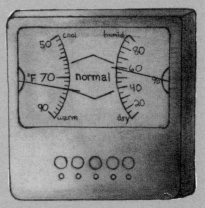

Hygrometers measure humidity and temperature, enabling you to determine the relative humidity in your home.

can be placed throughout the house to get an idea of the humidity levels in various areas. When testing, get a good overall representative reading by testing the air in the room and then the air right near the plant. Whenever you move the hygrometer, give it at least an hour to register the new temperature and humidity level.

drying winds blow through at times from October through March. Within an hour of the winds starting up, our humidity drops from 60% to 40%. Heating and air-conditioning also lower humidity. Even if the overall air moisture is sufficient, those plants sitting in the range of a heater or air-conditioning duct will suffer from dry air.

indoor gardening the organic way

HUMIDIFY ME, PLEASE

Besides moving yourself and your plants to the tropics, there are several ways to raise the humidity level of your home so that your plants are healthier and happier. Although your indoor garden would no doubt be in heaven, it's not necessary and sometimes not even practical to transform your home into a jungle with the use of humidifiers. Raising the humidity level in the plant's vicinity by even just a few degrees can make the difference.

One summer when temperatures continually reached the nineties in Southern California, my China Doll (*Radermachera sinica*), which had been happily growing in my home office for two years, began shedding leaves. I looked for pests, but there were none, so I decided to repot. When that didn't help, I tried fertilizer, but it still cried out for help. For a while, the plant was dropping leaves faster than I could pick them up, and I thought I might lose it. Eventually, after checking all other possibilities, I realized that the summer before hadn't been quite so hot and dry. As adaptable as it had been, my China Doll wanted more moisture. I began misting it on a regular basis, and it perked up within a week.

Misting your plants is only one of several things you can do to raise the humidity level for them. The following methods boost moisture levels. They can be used on their own or collectively, depending on the amount of humidity you're trying to create. The more methods you use, the higher your moisture level will be.

Misting

Although opinions vary on this topic, I've found that most houseplants—except for fuzzy-leaved ones such as African violets—like regular misting. Not only does it create a humid atmosphere, but it also lightly washes foliage and prevents overly dry conditions, which discourages pests such as spider mites.

The type of mister you use will be determined by the amount of misting you need to do. If you have a lot of plants to mist, a pump mister found at the nursery or hardware store is probably your best bet. Often used for dispensing liquid fertilizer and pesticides, they tend to have a large water-holding capacity and create a fine mist.

Misting temporarily increases the humidity around your houseplants.

misting basics

Using tepid or room temperature water, mist in the morning so that plants have time to dry out before night. Misting should create a fine fog of moisture that surrounds and covers each plant. Leaves should look as if light dew has settled on them. Some plants want daily misting; others are okay with two to three times a week. Experiment and see what works best for each plant.

Besides misting, it's also a good idea to gently rinse plants outside or in the bathtub at least twice a year. Or, if feasible, put them out in a gentle rain shower. Not only does washing them off raise the humidity level, it waters them, cleans plant leaves, and helps prevent spider mite infestations. When rinsing plants, tilt them at a 45° angle, if possible, which will ensure that any pests or their eggs rinse down the drain or onto the ground rather than into the soil.

If you will be spraying a small number of plants and don't wish to store a pump, a handheld water bottle will also work, as long as it can be adjusted to deliver a moist haze. Find such bottles in home improvement centers.

Humidity Tray

At the floor of the tropical rainforest where many houseplants call home, the thick humidity keeps plants content. To ensure that your own indoor collection stays happy, it's your job to replicate those steamer-like conditions. One of the best ways to do this is to create a humidity tray, which allows you to place plants above water. As the water evaporates, it humidifies the surrounding air and gives

creating a humidity tray

Make a humidity tray by filling a waterproof plate or bowl with polished stones, pebbles, or marbles. Be sure to use a tray or bowl made of plastic, glass, or glazed ceramic and not clay, which can "sweat" and damage surfaces. Add water to the container, stopping when the water level is just below the surface of the stones, pebbles or marbles. Place the plant on top of this, making sure that no water touches the bottom of the pot, as this can lead to root rot. Humidity created in the water below will continually rise to the plant. Check the effectiveness of your humidity tray by taking a reading near the plant with a hygrometer and compare to results taken a few feet away. Refill the tray when the water level gets low.

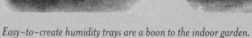

Easy-to-create humidity trays are a boon to the indoor garden.

Keep a humidity tray filled and the evaporating water will continually humidify the air surrounding your houseplant.

your houseplants extra moisture. It is also an excellent way to humidify plants that can't be misted because of fuzzy leaves susceptible to leaf spotting and rotting, such as African violets and purple velvet plant (*Gynura* sp.).

Grouping

When grouped, plants create a more humid environment for one another. Water evaporates from plant leaves during transpiration, which is the process by which plants cool off. This water vapor creates humidity around each transpiring plant. The more plants you put together, the more humidity they create for one another.

Group small plants, making sure to leave some room in between them for air circulation. Or try surrounding the base of larger plants with small ones.

WATCH YOUR TEMPERATURE

Although many houseplants have tropical origins, most do well in an average household temperature of 65°F to 75°F. Keep in mind that they don't appreciate surprises. The more stable the temperature remains, the happier your houseplants will be.

MULCH

Mulching your plants with moss will keep moisture in the air around the plant and raise humidity. This practice

gardening in miniature

One way to ensure the constant humidity and steady temperatures that many houseplants love is to create a terrarium. Aquariums, fishbowls, big wine bottles, and large jars make great miniature greenhouses. For a more stylish option, try a Wardian case. These decorative plant homes establish a striking focal point in the indoor garden. Generally crafted of metal, wood, and glass, they may also include a stand. Whatever you choose, use clear, rather than tinted, glass so that the terrarium receives adequate light and you can easily see your mini garden.

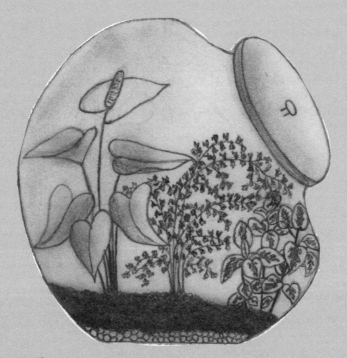

Terrariums are a fun way to grow a miniature moisture-loving garden.

When choosing a terrarium, keep in mind that the larger the opening, the easier to install and care for plants. An aquarium is a good choice for beginners.

Choose small, slow-growing plants that require similar growing requirements. Foliage plants are usually easiest, although some flowering varieties will do well. Avoid plants with fuzzy, thick leaves; their foliage holds too much water and they can rot. For the best visual effect, use plants of different sizes and heights and include some with variegated foliage.

High moisture lovers that can thrive in the closed moist quarters of a terrarium include ferns, spreading clubmosses like *Selaginella*, radiator plant (*Peperomia* species), maidenhair fern (*Adiantum* species), various gesneriads, nerve plant (*Fittonia verschaffeltii*), parlor palm (*Chamaedorea elegans*), miniature creeping fig (*Ficus pumila* 'Minima'), zebra plant, and *Anthurium*.

Before planting, create a ¾-inch layer of crushed gravel on the bottom of the Wardian case or terrarium. Next, sprinkle a ½-inch layer of slightly moistened charcoal chips, which will prevent odors from forming. Top this with two to three inches of a pre-moistened soil-less potting mix that contains coconut coir or peat moss and perlite or pumice. (The rich organic mix I generally recommend might lead to fungal problems in such a humid environment.)

Building a terrarium is a lot like making a tiny garden. Add visual interest by mounding the soil in some areas. Besides plants, include accessories such as polished stones, marbles, small mirrors, and miniature Christmas ornaments, which make great gazing balls. Doll furniture like tables and chairs and tiny garden tools also add a charming touch.

When planting is complete, mist the terrarium a little. If any soil has stuck to the sides, clean it off with a cloth. Keep the top open until there is no condensation on the glass, then cover. If you don't have a lid, terrariums can be covered with plastic wrap. After a day or two, check for condensation. Although you want some, excess can drip onto plants and rot them. Increase air circulation if this becomes a problem.

With their high humidity, terrariums require very little watering. Do so only when the top of the soil is dry. Keep things clean and remove ailing plants and fallen leaves immediately. Terrariums require a bright location but no direct sunlight, which can cook the interior of the greenhouse. When lighting is low, try fluorescent lighting (see chapter 5).

enhances the appearance of the plant and cuts down on watering. You can also create a mulch humidity tray by double potting your plant and placing moss in between the two pots. Routinely spray the moss with water, and it will release humidity to the plant.

CONSIDER LOCATION

Keep plants that like humidity out of all drafts because continuous air movement and sudden changes in temperature will dry them out. Position them away from windows, doors, and heating and air-conditioning ducts.

If the lighting is right, many plants can thrive in bathrooms and kitchens, which are naturally humid. Activities such as washing dishes and showering noticeably raise the humidity level for periods of time.

TRY LOW-HUMIDITY LOVERS

If providing your plants with sufficient moisture seems like too much work, try houseplants that like it dry. Top low moisture picks include succulents, such as snake plant (*Sansevieria trifasciata*), cactus, *Dracaena marginata*, fiddle-leaf fig (*Ficus lyrata*), pothos (*Epipremnum aureum*), ponytail plant (*Beaucarnea recurvata*), grape ivy (*Cissus rhombifolia*), radiator plant, cast-iron plant (*Aspidistra elatior*), wax plant (*Hoya carnosa*), and spider plant (*Chlorophytum comosum*).

TOO HUMID?

In all fairness to those readers who live in moist climes, it is possible to have too much humidity. Humidity itself isn't directly damaging, but it can encourage the development of molds, mildews, and other fungal diseases. Infected plants will show white or gray growths, rotted and mushy tissue, or discolored leaves (see chapter 8). Such problem areas should be removed immediately to prevent their spread.

When humidity is high, registering above 70% on the hygrometer, make sure that ventilation is excellent. Air movement will help prevent fungal infection outbreaks. Also consider that air-conditioning will dry out humid air—not to mention make an environment more comfortable!

7

keeping plants spiffy

We all like to look our best, and our foliage friends are no exception. Cleaning, pinching, pruning, and staking lead to healthier, more attractive houseplants.

GROOMING

Besides looking good, tidy plants make poor breeding grounds for pests and diseases. Taking a few moments to groom your plants gives you a chance to check for trouble and react quickly. Pests are attracted to yellow dying leaves and faded flowers. Mildews and molds tend to start in decaying foliage and then spread to healthier areas of the plant.

Sparkling plants also breathe well and are better able to clean the air. Anything that accumulates on foliage ultimately slows growth. Dust and other substances create a barrier between the leaves and sunlight, which is their source of energy and means of performing photosynthesis. Dust also blocks air, which interferes with transpiration. While plants are partly self-cleaning and can absorb some of the dust and grime from your home, they can't assimilate large amounts.

If your home is clean and dust isn't a problem on your plants, good for you—but take a close look just in case. You might be surprised to find how quickly dust and other substances pile up on plant leaves. I have a rubber plant in my bathroom that I clean on a regular basis. Not only does the dust build up, but it also gets splattered with toothpaste!

How often you must clean plant leaves depends on a variety of factors, including where you live and the plant's location in your home. In urban and industrial areas, you will need to dust plants more often. Plants in high activity rooms like the kitchen and bathroom require more frequent cleanings.

Rinsing is the easiest way to clean your small and medium-sized plants. Transport them to the sink and gently run water over the foliage. Small plants can even be picked up, turned over, and dunked completely in water. Secure the soil in place with a paper towel or rag and gently swirl the foliage for several seconds.

Larger plants that are more difficult to move can be cleaned in place. Wipe both sides of each leaf down with a damp cloth. Use a material that is soft so that you don't scratch the delicate leaf surface. To kill off any latent pests, add insecticidal soap to your cleaning water.

Though they are hard to move, it's generally a good idea to hose off large plants two to four times a year. This can

Avoid leaf shine products. Although they create a glossy sheen, they actually block the plant's stomata and cut off transpiration, as well as light. Would you want to put a coating of wax on your skin? Also stay away from homemade concoctions like beer, milk, cooking oil, and mayonnaise, which can all badly gum up plants, making them particularly difficult to clean and a magnet for pests and diseases.

be done in the shower. Just make sure that the showerhead sprays gently and that you use warm water. Tip the plant at a 45° angle, so the rinsing water washes into the tub rather than into the soil. You can also let nature do the dirty work and shower your plants in a gentle rainstorm. They'll return to the indoors clean and rejuvenated (see chapter 3 for how good rainwater is for your houseplants).

PINCHING AND PRUNING

Nature trims outdoor plants with strong winds, heavy rains, snow, and animals, but houseplants rely on you for a reg-

cleaning fuzzy-leaved plants

Plants like African violets and purple velvet plant have soft fuzzy leaves that usually don't respond well to being dunked or rinsed. They do require cleaning, however. For such plants, I suggest a soft moist rag or even dampened fingers. Wet your fingers and wipe off a leaf; then rinse and repeat.

ular "haircut." In time, many indoor plants outgrow their space or appear straggly and unbalanced. Pruning and pinching creates a healthy, attractive indoor garden by encouraging strong new growth and correcting structural problems. Done early enough, it will keep a plant the right size and shape for its space.

Pinching and pruning growing tips creates a more compact, fuller plant by stimulating dormant buds on a stem to grow. This prevents upright plants from shooting up and growing tall but sparse foliage and vining plants from becoming lanky. When pinching a hanging plant, keep a natural, uncut look by removing stems at uneven lengths. Although not all houseplants need pruning, most will benefit from some attention, even if it's simply removing dead leaves or diseased or damaged stems.

Pinch or cut judiciously. A good pruning job is barely noticeable. Keep in mind that unlike outdoor plants, houseplants are generally leisurely in their growth. It takes a long time for a major stem to be replaced, and in some cases it will never grow back. When in doubt, don't cut. If you come to a fork in the plant, so to speak, it's a good idea to take a break and come back to the pruning job with a fresh eye. At that point, you can usually see where the cuts should be made.

Light trimming and re-shaping can be done any time of the year, but more heavy pruning should be completed during spring or early fall. Plants tend to recover from surgery more quickly during the milder conditions of these seasons.

In general, there are two forms of trimming: pinching and pruning. Pinching is the gentlest form of cutting back and is used to guide plants in the right direction. Use this method on small, herbaceous plants with soft stems. Pinching doesn't correct structural or growing problems. It shapes a plant so that problems don't occur in the first place. You would pinch back a young pothos, for instance, to keep it dense and shapely.

Pinching

Always pinch just above a leaf node (where there is a leaf or a bump in the foliage). New growth will come from that node. Pinching close to the node is important because any bare stem left will die back and rot, and excess stem can cause a node not to activate and grow.

Most growing tips are tender, so your thumb and forefinger make adequate pinchers. If not, use pruners or a sharp knife. Avoid leaving any jagged stem tips, which can attract disease.

Some plants require regular pinching, while others only need it once or twice a year. Use care when pinching plants that flower so that you don't cut off any buds. Get to know the flowering cycle of your plant before doing any pinching.

Plants such as African violets send up leaves from a flat crown and generally have a round symmetrical shape called a rosette. Such plants only need pruning to maintain an even shape. Remove older leaves from the underside of the

plants to pinch regularly

Plants that require pinching:

- Arrowhead vine (*Syngonium podophyllum*)
- *Begonia* (various)
- Bloodleaf (*Iresine herbstii*)
- Coleus x hybridus
- Goldfish plant (*Columnea* species)
- Grape ivy (*Cissus rhombifolia*)
- Philodendron (*P. scandens*)
- Lipstick plant (*Aeschynanthus* species)
- Nerve plant (*Fittonia verschaffeltii*)
- Polka-dot plant (*Hypoestes phyllostachya*)
- Pothos (*Epipremnum aureum*)
- Purple velvet plant (*Gynura* species)
- Radiator plant (*Peperomia* species)
- Wandering Jew (*Tradescantia zebrina/Zebrina pendula*)
- Wax plant (*Hoya carnosa*)

rosette, pinching off the leaf and its petiole as close to the base as you can. You should also remove any leaves that are misshapen or that make the plant appear unbalanced.

When pruning a houseplant, cut at an angle just above a leaf node. New growth will come from the exposed leaf node.

Pruning

Pruning is often a reaction to a problem that has occurred over time such as an overly long branch or long, straggly stems. You may also want to shape a plant or reduce its height. Houseplants that tend to require pruning include large, woody plants, like *Ficus benjamina*, *Schefflera* species, dumb cane, various dracaenas, and some flowering plants.

General Pruning Guidelines:

1. Always cut at an angle just above a node, which is where a branch or leaf is or was attached. There are dormant buds at each node and cutting at that point will stimulate one or more replacement stems to grow from the exposed node. Use high-quality bypass pruners. Avoid anvil cutters, as they tend to crush the stem rather than provide a clean cut. Uneven cuts attract bacteria and pests.

2. Remove and destroy dead or diseased stems, cutting them off flush with the main stem or branch.

3. Trim according to a plant's natural growth habit. You want the plant to be a pleasing shape when you're done. Shorten leggy stems areas that have gone awry. Also remove any interior crossing branches.

4. When shaping a large plant, proceed slowly and step back periodically to view your handiwork.

5. To ensure that you get as many blooms as possible from flowering plants, prune or pinch right after a bloom cycle. This will stimulate them to rebloom more quickly and prevents unwittingly removing buds. Prune lipstick plant and goldfish plant back by one-third after flowering. Remove flower stalks from African violets, begonias, gloxinias, peace lilies, wax plant, and zebra plant when they are finished.

6. When shortening a dracaena such as corn plant, cut the cane at an angle to prevent water from settling on the stump. Depending on the size of the cane you cut down, one to three or four side shoots will come up and begin growing, making it a shorter, bushier plant. You can also get a whole new plant when you prune by airlayering (see chapter 10).

7. If the plant you're pruning is fleshy, like dumb cane, rubber tree, or various dracaenas, it's advisable to treat the cuts. Let them callus overnight and then dust with ground cinnamon the next day. Cinnamon has antibacterial properties and will help prevent the growth of bacteria that could lead to rotting. Barkier plants like *Ficus benjamina* don't require cinnamon treatment, although it's natural and won't harm any plant, so when in doubt, use it.

SUPPORT

At some point, we all need support. And some of us need more than others. The same goes for houseplants. While some indoor plants have strong stems and readily grow without any staking or a trellis on which to cling, others need quite a bit of bracing to grow well and look their best. Keep in mind that indoor plants are sheltered from strong winds, which are responsible in the outdoor environment for strengthening plant stems.

There are several reasons to support a plant. Staking helps unsteady plants and floppy flowerheads stand up straight. Strategically placed supports can also train plants to grow in a particular direction. (In such cases, stakes are often used to correct a problem and can be removed at a later date.) How much support a plant requires depends on its growth habits. In their native habitat, some plants naturally grow on trees and other woody plants. Trellising can give such plants the comforts of home. Young plants usually take readily to staking, while older plants may not be so compliant.

Plants that benefit from some type of support fall into three categories. First, there are plants with flowers that look best when displayed upright, such as orchids. Insert a stake in the soil near the plant base and secure the plant's main stem to the stake with green garden tape. This can be found at nurseries and home supply stores and is your best option when tying all plants. Garden tape is plastic and stretches as the plant grows. Using items such as string or fishing line is not advisable. Such products can cut stems or, in a worst-case scenario, girdle a trunk and kill a plant. When green garden tape isn't strong enough—such as for large trees—use twine, but protect the branch or trunk with a buffer, such as a piece of carpeting or foam.

Ramblers, trailers, and climbers form the second category of plants that benefit from staking. With a little direction and something to attach to such as a trellis system, these plants can be trained to grow wherever you desire.

making a moss-covered pole

Although you can find moss-covered poles in the nursery, they may not be tall enough or very absorbent, so I suggest making your own. To do so, take a piece of plastic PVC pipe and wrap it with moist sphagnum moss. (Always use gloves when handling wet sphagnum, as it harbors a fungus that can be harmful to the skin.) Fasten the moss to the pole with fine wire, such as 24-gauge copper wire or fishing line. Wrap the wire around the entire length of the pole and secure both ends. Leave the top portion of the moss pole open so that you can insert additional plastic tubing if the plant outgrows the pipe; into the bottom of the pole insert a plant stake, which will allow you to secure the pole in the pot.

Once you've created the moss pole, soak it for several hours and make sure that it's saturated before using it. Insert into the pot as near to the base of the plant as you can without harming roots. Keep the moss constantly moist by spraying on a regular basis. Don't let it dry out completely, as it will be difficult to re-wet without re-soaking—a difficult thing to do once a plant is happily attached.

Creating your own moss pole for climbing plants such as philodendron is easy.

Obvious candidates include arrowhead vine, wax plant, pothos, wandering Jew, and various ivies.

The third group of plants have aerial roots and grow best when allowed to fasten and climb onto a continuously moist, moss-covered pole. Two plant types that fall into this category include the split-leaf philodendron and the trailing or vining philodendron.

Stakes and trellises can be found in nurseries or home supply stores and come in a wide variety of styles and sizes.

You'll find everything from single stakes to heart-shaped trellises. Materials also vary. Bamboo, wood, metal, wire, and plastic are common.

When selecting a plant support, consider the plant and the size and style of your container. Single stakes are best for single-stemmed plants. Climbing multi-branching house-plants generally require some sort of a trellis, either rigid like metal or pliable like wire. You can even insert a variety of stakes into the sides of a pot, pull them together, and secure them at the top to create a tepee-like support. Durable metal supports are heaviest, while bamboo and wood tend to be the most lightweight, although they will deteriorate over time. The rule of thumb is to choose a stake that is at least the diameter of the stem of the plant you are staking. Thin stakes tend to bend and can break.

There are small plastic and wood trellis supports made specifically for indoor plants, but vining and climbing plants often outgrow them quickly. It's often best to use a larger, taller out-door trellis. Be aware that the weight of a plant fastened to a trellis or stake may cause it to fall over. Such top-heavy conditions can be dealt with in one of two

Tepee-type supports work well for vining and climbing plants.

Create your own plant supports exactly to your specifications. They can easily be made from disease-free twigs and branches collected from the outdoor garden. A good time to do this is in the fall and winter months when you can find deciduous prunings. Such new cuttings are moist and pliable and can be fashioned into just about any shape you desire. Tie them and they will keep their new shape when they dry. Some good plant prunings to use include peach, plum, apricot, and apple tree branches and wisteria and grape vines.

ways. First, you can mulch with pebbles, which will give the plant more stability. If that doesn't provide sufficient support, put the plant into a heavy ceramic cachepot, and for extra weight, add rocks to the base of the cachepot. (You need a humidity tray anyway).

CLIMB THE WALLS

For an especially stunning look, you can train vining and trailing plants to climb the expanse of a wall or even the ceiling. Creeping fig actually attaches itself to walls in a barnacle fashion, but most climbers need some help. You can secure a wall trellis to your wall, or insert nails or screws every few inches and cover this with plastic trellising. You can also run twine from the floor to the ceiling, and train plants to climb it. Keep in mind that such plantings become a permanent fixture in the room. They are difficult to repot, although it can be done with some care. Repotting must be done in place, and it may require that you break or cut the existing pot so that you can install the rootball into a bigger container. Delay the tricky chore of repotting as long as possible by making sure that the plant is in a pot that is big enough to begin with. Topdressing also helps (see chapter 9) to prolong the time in between repotting.

Other plants that do well on a wall trellis include trailing or vining philodendron, pothos, wax plant, and various ivies.

It's best to install stakes and trellises before planting, but that's not always possible. Minimize root damage by inserting supports with care and placing them as deep as possible within the container. This will help secure the plant in the pot and prevent it from tumbling over. Insert the stakes as unobtrusively as possible. Try to camouflage them among foliage. Use stakes that are green or bark colored and tie with green garden tape, which tends to blend in. Always secure the plant to the stake in two or three spots so that it isn't vulnerable to breaking in any particular area. As you stake, keep in mind the plant's natural growth pattern.

8

dealing with pesky critters and diseases

Houseplants are like children. No matter how good a parent you are, they eventually get sick. And yes, even the best indoor gardeners have trouble with pests and diseases. My nemesis is the mealybug. The furry white fiend pops up throughout my indoor garden even in the best of times, and it has since I started indoor gardening at the age of eight.

When you find scale on your *Ficus benjamina* or fungus root gnats buzzing around your African violets, don't panic. Yes, pests are annoying, and yes, they do cause damage, but they're also a natural part of the plant world and just doing their job. There are many reasons that we ought to thank them. The goal of pests and diseases is targeting dead and dying plant matter and returning it to the soil. Pests can be an indicator that you've got a cultural problem or a nutritional deficiency that should be addressed.

Change your perception about pests and diseases, and it's easier to deal with them.

Considering that pests are a natural part of your indoor mini-ecosystem, it's easy to see the problem with mass annihilation pushed by the chemical insecticide and pesticide industry. Until recently, pesticides and insecticides have been the treatment of choice since their widespread use began in the 1930s. Most people have been trained to fear and dread all bugs and are encouraged to blast anything that moves. After application, things do become eerily quiet for a while, but it's a lot like a B-rated horror flick. The pests you thought you got rid of become resistant to the insecticide and come back—only worse. You've also killed off more fragile beneficial insects that are happy to feed on bad bugs, if you'd only let them. Use systemic pesticides, which give a plant a continuous dose of poison, and you might manage to keep pests at bay, but you'll weaken the plant overall.

The message that broad-spectrum chemical pest controls are harmful to the outdoor environment has become widely accepted. Many home gardeners now use less toxic methods of fighting pests in the yard. Spraying anything that moves indoors is still considered your best option, however, which truly amazes me. How is it that we're eating organic foods, using natural personal care products, cleaning our indoor air, yet we still blast our poor houseplants with toxic chemicals? You'd actually be better off using pesticides outdoors where air movement and rain carry away toxic residues. Indoor plants, on the other hand, are captive in their pots. The bottle of insecticide may say that the product wears off in a certain amount of time, but be assured, it will linger for months and possibly years in your soil unless you repot.

I'm not saying all of this to shame or scare you. If you've used pesticides on your houseplants, it's possible to reverse the damage. First, though, swear as a now-informed plant parent that you'll only use organic, less toxic tactics in the future. Your aim should not be complete eradication. It's not possible or practical, and it's certainly not healthy for you or your plants. The key is to live with tolerable pest levels, which is possible if you take a kinder, gentler approach.

BENEFICIAL INSECTS/BIOCONTROLS

Did you know that most bugs are actually good guys? Did you also know that all bad bugs have at least one, if not many, natural predators? It's actually possible to introduce good bugs into your home. Greenhouses have successfully used such biocontrols for years. I have beneficial insects in my indoor garden, including ladybugs. Not only do they snack on troublemakers like mealybugs, but ladybugs are also a delightful addition to the indoor garden and make for great conversation when guests drop by.

Beneficial insects are generally divided into two categories: predators and parasites. The ladybug (ladybird beetle) is probably the most recognizable predator. It and its larvae, which resemble alligators with black and orange spots, greedily feed on a variety of soft-bodied houseplant pests, including aphids, mealybugs, and spider mites.

Beneficial parasites, on the other hand, don't directly consume a pest. Instead, they take up residence inside of an unwanted bug, feeding off of its innards as they reproduce. A good example is the mealybug parasite *Leptomastix dactylopii*. This tiny wasp lays its eggs inside of mealybugs. When the eggs hatch, the wasp larvae completely consume the mealybug.

Beneficial predators and parasites are most effective in the indoor garden when the infestation isn't too heavy. If the pest population is high, first knock it down with one of the non-toxic eradication methods mentioned below and then introduce beneficial insects.

NON-TOXIC OPTIONS

Isopropyl Alcohol

Most indoor pests will dry and shrivel up when sprayed or dabbed with good old rubbing alcohol. It leaves no residue and is my weapon of choice with mealybugs, as it penetrates their protective waxy coating and dries them up. I generally apply rubbing alcohol at full strength and have never damaged any plants. If you are concerned about leaf damage, however, test it on one leaf first. You can also dilute it to half water and half alcohol.

Soap Sprays

There are a variety of products on the market designed to suffocate pests. These products contain vegetable fatty acids, and sticking and spreading agents. While recipes to make your own soap spray exist, it's important to understand that the bonds in dish soap alone aren't strong enough to thoroughly coat an insect and suffocate it. Once the pest moves, the bonds are broken and the pest can breathe. With vegetable fatty acids in the mix, the bonds are strong enough to stay linked and put an end to the pest. Many soap sprays also have added botanical pesticides such as pyrethrin or neem (discussed below).

Neem Oil

It is a wonder cure for many pests and diseases. Its active ingredient, azadirachtin, is pressed from the seed of the neem tree (*Azadirachta indica*), which is native to eastern India and Burma. For centuries, neem leaves, stems, seeds, and oil have been used for medicinal purposes and pest control in India. Many tests have found neem oil to be an effective insecticide, miticide, and fungicide. It is also an appetite suppressant that discourages insects from feeding on plants, and it inhibits insect mating and reduces female fertility. Perhaps best of all, neem doesn't usually harm beneficials. It generally affects only those insects that feed on sprayed plants, and most beneficial insects feed on the pests themselves. Neem oil in an ultrafine form has also been shown to effectively fight foliar fungal infections and to suffocate spider mites and their eggs.

One particularly effective product, known as BioNeem, causes appetite suppression in insects and contains a growth regulator. It makes pests such as aphids, thrips, and white-flies stop producing and starve to death.

Ultra-Fine Horticultural Oils

They suffocate a wide variety of unsuspecting pests and their eggs, such as spider mites, scale, mealybugs, and aphids. Unlike versions from years past used as dormant sprays, today's ultra-fine oils can be applied at any time of the year. Some are petroleum-based, while others are made from pressed and squeezed cottonseed oil. Horticultural oil should be made fresh each time you use it, as old mix can burn plants.

Manual Removal

Some pests can be removed or destroyed with a cloth or even your fingers. This is an especially effective method for scale.

Water

A good blast or rinsing with water will often knock off a majority of pests, leaving the plant less stressed. This is often your best first step when an infestation is high. Take the plant to the sink or shower and rinse pests down the drain. Follow with another non-toxic removal method until things are under control.

Yellow Sticky Traps

Yellow sticky traps are bright yellow traps pre-coated with a sticky substance that stops and traps flying pests like fungus root gnats, thrips, and some aphids. Yellow is used because most insects are drawn to it. Not only does this rid your indoor garden of troublemakers, it can tip you off early before an infestation occurs. Reapply sticky material when the trap is full or replace the trap.

Botanical Pesticides

Botanical pesticides come from plant material. The active ingredients in these sprays are extracted directly from flowers, leaves, bark, or roots and break down to harmless compounds within a few days. Many will, however, harm beneficial insects, so I recommend using them only as a last resort when infestations are high.

One strong yet effective botanical insecticide is pyrethrin, which is derived from the dried powdered flowers of the pyrethrum daisy. Pyrethrins, which are mainly concentrated in the seeds of the flower head, are a contact insecticide, which means the insect need only touch the substance to be affected. Pyrethrins damage insect neurosystems and paralyze them. While this botanical control

buyer beware

A word of warning: Carefully read labels and examine active ingredients, which you should recognize. Petrochemical companies have devised products that look and sound like natural pest solutions but that are actually very nasty chemical controls. Some packages say pyrethroid, for instance, which is a synthetic version of pyretherin.

is strong, it is quickly destroyed by heat and light, so there are no residual effects.

Common Foods

When mixed with ultra-fine horticultural oils or neem, baking soda is a good control for fungal disease on leaves. Follow the directions for the oil product and add one to two tablespoons of baking soda per gallon of mix. Various beneficial bacteria in raw milk have also shown to fight powdery mildew.

You can minimize and even prevent pest infestations and some diseases by giving your plants a healthy, organic life, which will give them the strength and vigor to fight off pests and diseases. It's a lot like the healthy person who eats plenty of nutritious foods, drinks lots of

it's not your fault

Ever get a houseplant home, only to have it drop dead a few weeks or even a month or two later? Don't blame yourself too quickly. The problem with your failed houseplant may have occurred because of a bad "childhood" experience.

As humans it's hard for us to understand that commercial houseplants are often produced in an inhumane, high-volume way. The goal is to sell them as quickly as possible, so when they have a problem like a bacterial disease, it's treated with antibacterials instead of dealing with the bacterial problem itself. Many houseplants show problems such as root rot after someone brings them home because treatment has stopped.

water, and stays well groomed. Such a person is more likely to fight off illness.

REACT QUICKLY

If and when a plant does fall victim to pests or disease, how you react at the first sign of trouble is the key to whether your plant will develop a full-blown disease or snap back to health quickly. Early detection of pests on houseplants is critical. Learn what the insects look like and where they congregate (see below). Because some pests, like spider mites and thrips, are small, inspect your plants with a 10× hand lens or a high-quality magnifying glass.

General signs that a plant is in trouble due to insect damage or disease include droopy leaves despite wet soil; sticky residue on plant leaves or around pots; reduced, distorted, or shriveled new growth; foliage loss; stunting and failure to thrive; small black or white dots or brown or black splotches on leaves; and overall change in color. Also trust a gut feeling that something is wrong.

If you do see a pest problem, it is critical that you act fast.

- Isolate problem plants immediately to prevent their spreading the insect or disease to others in your foliage family.
- Once you decide on an organic method of treatment, remember that multiple applications are often necessary for control. Have patience and be consistent.

- Check other plants for the pest.
- Recheck treated plants on a periodic basis to make sure that the pest hasn't returned. Some pests can leave eggs behind, which will eventually hatch and cause new problems.

THE PESKIEST OF PESTS AND DISEASES AND HOW TO GET RID OF THEM

Insect pests love to feed on tender houseplant growth. Here are the top seven villains and how to treat them if your plants succumb.

Aphids

Aphids

These small, fleshy insects come in many colors, including yellow, red, black, brown, and green. They generally cluster and feed on new plant growth, sucking plant sap out of leaves, which will lead to leaf holes and distortion or stunting of new growth. Plant vigor is also reduced. While feeding, they excrete a sticky honeydew liquid, which can drop on furniture or other leaves and attract black sooty mold. Aphids are active during the warm months when they reproduce quickly. Requiring no fertilization from a male, female aphids give birth to up to 12 live young per day.

Best non-toxic treatment methods: Water, hand removal, insecticidal soap spray, alcohol, pyrethrin.

Biocontrol options: Green lacewing adults and larvae, ladybugs.

Fungus Root Gnats

The larvae of this common indoor pest look like small grubs with transparent milky white bodies and shiny black heads. Adults resemble small mosquitoes and can be annoying as they buzz around the house, often stopping to hover in front of your face. It's the larvae, however, that cause the most damage. They thrive in moist soil conditions and feed on decaying plant material and plant roots. Badly infested specimens wilt, roots may rot, and the plant can become disfigured. The cycle con-

Fungus Root Gnats

tinues as the adults feed on microscopic fungi at the top of the soil and then lay their eggs. Fungus root gnats are especially a problem in organic gardens because the adults and larvae prefer humus-rich soil.

Best non-toxic treatment methods: Trap adults with

yellow sticky traps. Eliminate overly moist conditions, which the larvae need to survive, by letting the soil of the infected plant dry out some. This will cause the larvae to die and will dry up the fungi at the top of the soil that the adults feed on. If possible, wait until the top inch or two of soil is dry and the plants are flagging (see chapter 3). Increasing air movement also helps to reduce the growth of fungi on the soil surface.

Biocontrol options: The fungus gnat mite (*Hypoaspis*) is a tiny brown mite that is found naturally in the top layer of soil where fungus gnat, as well as thrip larvae, dwell. The female *Hypoaspis* lays her eggs in the soil, and the resulting nymphs and adults feed on the fungus root gnat's larvae.

The predatory nematodes *Steinernema carpocapsae* and *Steinernema feltiae* also do a great job of controlling fungus root gnats. Nematodes are tiny parasitic roundworms that kill their hosts rapidly by invading their bodies. When inside, they release a bacteria that poisons the blood of the host. The nematode then reproduces inside the dead insect and the process begins again. These nematodes are easy to find and are cost effective. They tend to remain in the soil even when fungus root gnat larvae isn't present, which makes them a good preventative. An application in spring and the beginning of winter is recommended.

Mealybugs

These white, cottony pests suck sap from plant leaves and produce a sticky residue that can attract black sooty mold.

They thrive in tight areas on plants, such as cracks and crevices where leaves attach to the stem and in leaves that have not yet unfurled. Although they move slowly, if left unchecked, they will weaken and eventually kill a plant. Eliminating them often takes several attempts, as their cottony outsides act as an impenetrable barrier and they protect their eggs by laying them underneath themselves.

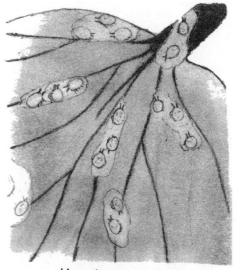

Mealybugs

Best non-toxic treatment methods: Alcohol spray or oil spray. After spraying, wait 30 minutes and then remove the treated mealybugs with a cotton swab or by rinsing the affected plant in the sink. This will expose any egg casings, which aren't visible to the naked eye. Spray and rinse again. Repeat every two to three days for two weeks, and then as needed.

Biocontrol options: The ladybug known as the crypt (*Cryptolaemus montrouzieri*) was imported from Australia in the 1890s. This hungry predator has a black body and a reddish head, abdomen, and tail segment. Familiarize yourself with this beneficial insect's larvae, which does most of the work. It is covered with thick, white, waxy filaments and resembles an oversized mealybug.

The mealybug parasite *Leptomastix dactylopii* also does a good job of ferreting out certain mealybugs. This tiny wasp lays its eggs inside of mealybugs, and when the eggs hatch, the wasp larvae completely consume the mealybug.

Scale

These smooth, brown, oval pests look like small, shiny bumps. They attach themselves to the underside of leaves

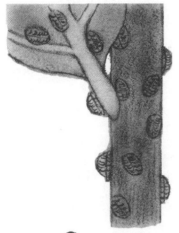

along the leaf midrib or onto stems. They will cause yellow leaves, leaf drop, and a sticky secretion that will attract black sooty mold. Eventually, they will kill a plant.

Best non-toxic treatment methods: Manual removal, oils, insecticidal soap spray, alcohol.

Biocontrol options: The readily available and very effective red scale exterminator (*Aphytis melinus*) is a parasitic wasp that lays up to 25 eggs underneath female scales. The *Aphytis* larvae then eats the soft underside of the scale insect and kills it. The purple scale parasite (*Rhizobius [Lindorus] lophanthae*) is a small black lady beetle that preys on both the larvae and the adult scales. *Rhizobius* can clean up large populations of scale and are very opportunistic, eating other pests as well, such as mealybugs.

Spider Mites

Spider mites, which are technically spiders and not mites, are usually found on the undersides of leaves, where they

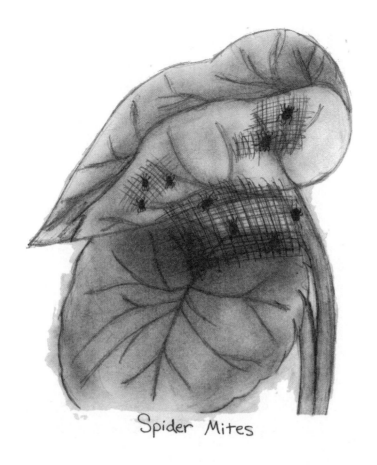

Spider Mites

create fine white webbing. They also suck leaf cells dry, producing yellow, speckled feeding marks. Leaf drop is common. When conditions are hot and dry, they are especially a problem. These extremely small spiders can only be seen with a hand lens.

Best non-toxic treatment methods: Water, insecticidal soap spray, oils (the latter is the only method that will kill eggs). Also increase humidity, as mites thrive in dry conditions.

Biocontrol options: There are several varieties of biological control species for spider mites, depending on temperature and humidity. The most aggressive biocontrol for the spider mite is the predatory mite *Phytoseiulus persimilis*, which eats about five to ten adults and twenty eggs a day. It does best in humid climates, but it can often find conditions moist enough right up next to the plant where it tends to stay. There are also *Neoseiulus californicus*, which require 60°F to 85°F and like 60% humidity, and the high heat and humidity lover *Galendromus occidentalis*, which can take up to 100°F and prefers at least 50% humidity.

Thrips

Thrips are tiny, but they do a great deal of damage. Using a hand lens or magnifying glass, look for small, long-bodied insects with fringed wings scurrying about. Also inspect for shiny black spots, which are fecal matter. Thrips feed on plant tissue, which causes silvering and mottling of stems, foliage, and flowers, the latter of which tend not to

Thrips

open. They are usually present in large numbers and can often be seen hopping around the plant. They pupate in the soil, so that should be treated as well.

Best non-toxic treatment methods: Increase humidity, as thrips thrive in dry conditions. Also try water, blue sticky traps (research shows they prefer the color blue), alcohol, insecticidal soap spray, and oil sprays (BioNeem).

Biocontrol options: Predatory nematodes *Steinernema carpocapsae* and *Steinernema feltiae* do a good job of getting rid of thrip larvae, which congregate on top of the soil. For leaf control, try the minute pirate bug (*Orius insidiosis*). This eye-catching bug will attack all stages of thrips and can eat 20 a day and kill even more. The thrip predator mite *Amblyseius cucumeris* will eat thrip larvae and eggs off leaf tissue.

Whiteflies

Whiteflies are minute insects that resemble tiny moths with wings covered in a white, waxy powder. They can become serious pests on some plants, particularly citrus, sucking sap from the leaves and causing plant decline. Larvae tend to feed at the bottom of the plant and adults toward the top.

Best non-toxic treatment methods: Sticky traps, insecticidal soap, alcohol spray, oils, pyrethrin.

Biocontrol options: The readily available parasitic wasp, *Encarsia formosa*, does an excellent job of controlling whitefly. These predators lay eggs in the third and fourth stages of the whitefly and feed on the first and second

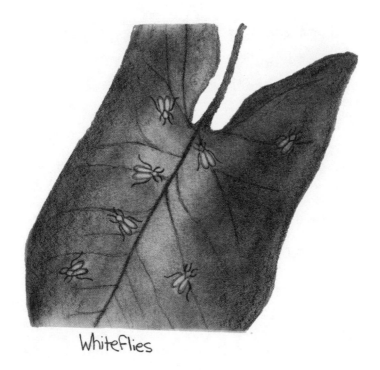

Whiteflies

stages, enabling them to wipe out entire populations. Lady-bugs also eat whitefly larvae.

COMMON DISEASES AND WHAT TO DO ABOUT THEM

Although there are no biocontrols for diseases, there are some preventative measures and various treatment methods. When spraying anything on plant leaves, always test a small area first.

Root and Crown Rot

The most common disease found in houseplants is root rot (Phythium), which generally occurs from overwatering or

indoor gardening the organic way

tip-burn

Though it may look like a disease, browning tips of otherwise healthy house-plant leaves indicates one or more of the following: (1) uneven watering or a sensitivity to certain substances in the water such chlorine, fluoride, or sodium; (2) overfeeding; (3) overly dry air; and/or (4) incorrect pH.

Solving the brown leaf dilemma takes (1) watering properly and using reverse osmosis or distilled water; (2) fertilizing correctly; (3) providing adequate humidity; and (4) adjusting pH as needed.

While you are rectifying matters, if the brown leaf tips bother you and to prevent insects and diseases from using the leaf as a breeding ground, simply cut the brown parts off, creating a shape that looks natural.

improper watering. Soil that is constantly wet, letting a pot sit in a saucer full of water, and heavy potting soil can lead to this condition. Signs that roots are in bad shape include reduced plant growth, fungus or brown areas on the leaves, and saggy foliage despite wet soil. Brown, squishy roots that are sometimes foul-smelling are also an indication. Healthy roots are usually firm and have an earthy smell.

Cultural preventions: Avoid root rot by only watering when the top one to two inches of soil is dry. Never let a pot sit in excess water in the drainage dish and don't compact the soil when potting.

Root Rot Symptoms

Best non-toxic treatment methods: Let soil dry out well between waterings. You can also try repotting the plant, rinsing as much soil from the roots as possible, and then using a peroxide rinse, which will kill bacteria. Mix one gallon of water with two teaspoons of peroxide and pour over plant roots. Then repot in a humus-rich soil (see chapter 9) and water with compost tea to reintroduce beneficial bacteria (see chapter 4). The latter will act as a buffer against harmful bacteria.

Powdery Mildew and Leaf Spot

Powdery mildew and leaf spot are fungal diseases that occur when conditions are overly moist at the root zone or on the leaves. Such diseases often occur when plants are stressed in terms of cultural conditions. Temperatures and humidity may be high and ventilation may be poor or foliage may be perpetually wet.

Leaf Spot

Leaf Spot

Leaf spot shows up on plants as small, soft brown spots and is common on dumb cane (*Dief-fenbachia* hybrids) and some dracaenas. It is generally a sign that cultural practices need adjustment. Leaf spot commonly occurs when plants are misted and the water stays on the leaf, stagnating and promoting bacteria or fungus. It may also happen in response to too little light and/or poor air circulation.

Cultural preventions: Remove affected leaf parts and dispose of them in a sealed plastic bag, as spores will travel to healthy leaves. Also increase air circulation, lower humidity, and check that lighting is sufficient. Mist early in the day and avoid doing so on moist days. Make certain that misting water dries up within five to ten minutes.

Best non-toxic treatment options: Leaf spot can be effectively controlled by spraying the leaves with ultra-fine oil or neem oil mixed with 2 teaspoons of baking soda. Though this treatment will not eliminate leaf spots that are already on the plant, it will prevent new spots from appearing.

Powdery Mildew

Powdery mildew tends to be host specific, only affecting a few indoor plants such as begonias, grape ivy (*Cissus rhombifolia*), and some succulents. It is comprised of parasitic organisms that coat leaves with a gray or white downy substance. The growth obstructs light and causes the leaves to curl up and fall off.

Cultural preventions: Remove all infected leaves. Lower the humidity and increase ventilation. Avoid watering the leaves and don't mist them.

Best non-toxic treatment options: Control powdery mildew by spraying the leaves with ultra-fine oil or neem oil mixed with 2 teaspoons of baking soda. Treatment will prevent new mildew from appearing.

LETTING GO

Sometimes saving a plant isn't possible or practical. When your indoor garden has become a hospital, it's often time to do some tossing. Throwing a plant away may be hard because it's a living thing, but it's often the best thing to do for the rest of your plants.

9

painless repotting

Houseplants are the forgiving sort. They must be to grow happily in the same pots year after year. They're also intelligent plants. Most have adapted to thrive in cramped quarters. You may get limited new growth and ailing health, however, if your indoor plants have sat in the same containers for several years. Houseplants eventually become root-bound, when the pot is so full of roots that plants have no more space in which to grow. It's not always cramped roots that make repotting necessary. The soil may be high in soluble salts or the pH too high or too low. Whatever the reason, repotting invigorates plants and ensures continued healthy growth.

Houseplants can be repotted throughout the year, but late winter through summer are the best times, as they are more actively growing during these periods. The ideal time is when the plant is just starting a growth cycle. I wouldn't recommend repotting during winter in most cases, because in cold and damp weather, soil tends to stay moist and you run the risk of fungal disease setting in. Wait until late winter when spring is around the corner.

Though you may have plants that haven't been repotted in years, time doesn't matter in the world of repotting. When to repot varies widely and depends on how quickly a plant grows. Most houseplants like to be crowded and only need repotting when they've become root-bound or the soil is salty or unbalanced.

Repot when you see one or more of the following:

1. Roots emerging from the bottom of the pot or a bulky mass of tangled roots in the container and very little soil. (If possible, remove the plant from the container and inspect the roots).
2. Constant thirst and soil that dries out quickly.
3. Water rushing through the pot when the plant is watered.
4. Sluggish growth.
5. Top-heaviness indicating that the plant has become too big for the pot. The plant should comprise no more than two-thirds of the plant-pot combination.
6. White staining on the soil surface, encircling the inside of the pot rim, and/or around the drainage holes, which indicates salt build-up. If the pot is terra-cotta, you'll also see white staining on the outside of the container.
7. A pH reading indicating that conditions aren't appropriate for that particular plant.

CHOOSING A NEW POT

Besides which houseplants to grow in your home, the second most important decision you'll make is what to grow them in. Remember that this is their home, so treat the decision carefully. Container choices vary widely, from terracotta to decorated ceramic pots to practical plastic to brass and wicker.

The type of pot you choose depends on the plant and its growing requirements, including how often it needs watering. You'll also want to choose a container that blends well with your decor. For instance, an orchid in an elegant metal pot works well for a contemporary interior, while a basket filled with a green and yellow croton lights up a cottage-style home. There are so many containers available, you're sure to find one that fits your home's style.

Also known as terra-cotta pots, clay containers are easy to find and come in many sizes and colors. There is the traditional terra-cotta color as well as brown, gold, green, red, and purple. Styles also vary. There are pots with built-in designs and planters shaped like frogs, fish, turtles, cats, and other animals.

Clay pots are porous and breathe, so they're your best choice for plants like orchids and succulents that require excellent drainage and a lot of air to the roots. They do dry out quickly, however, and require more frequent watering. It's important to protect furniture and flooring when using them because even if they don't have drainage holes, they aren't waterproof and can stain surfaces. Place terra-cotta pots on wrought-iron plant stands or cork or plastic furniture protectors. Another drawback of terra-cotta is that unsightly salt and mineral deposits accumulate on the outside of the pots, appearing as white markings. Occasional leaching of pots may remove such stains (see chapter 3). Clay pots also tend to be very dry when new. Before repotting, saturate the pot by soaking in water for 20 minutes to prevent the container from absorbing water from the potting soil.

Ceramic pots are close cousins to clay. Clay pots are usually only fired once in a kiln, which simply removes water from the clay and hardens the pot; ceramic pottery, on the other hand, is fired once, painted with glaze, and fired again. The second firing melts the glaze (which usually contains glass) onto the pot, creating a shiny, waterproof surface. These containers also come in an abundance of colors, styles, and designs. High quality ceramic pots that have no drainage holes make good cachepots, which refers to a decorative outer container designed to hold an inner pot. Ceramic containers also tend to be heavy and anchor top-heavy plants.

I'm not a huge fan of things in the home decor realm that are plastic, but I make an exception with plastic pots. In the last 10 years or so, plastic containers have sprouted up in dozens of colors, sizes, and styles, and many don't even look like plastic. Such pots have a variety of benefits including the fact that they are lightweight yet very sturdy. Plastic pots are also not porous and retain moisture, which means that plants require less frequent watering. They are an excellent choice for hanging plants and those that fruit and flower. However, because moisture generally only escapes from the soil surface in plastic pots, it's important to make sure that you don't overwater them. Plastic pots with drainage holes are often a good choice as inner containers within cachepots.

Fiberglass is another material being used to make containers. It is lightweight like plastic and very durable.

Metal pots and wicker baskets should only be used as cachepots. Line them with plastic to protect their interiors.

WATCH DRAINAGE

Good drainage is critical so that soil doesn't become waterlogged. Plastic pots should have several holes. If they don't, drill more. Terra-cotta and ceramic pots tend to have fewer holes. This is generally okay with clay pots because they breathe. Ceramic pots are often best used as cachepots.

SIZE MATTERS

When repotting, select a pot that is no more than one pot size up, which translates to no more than two inches bigger in circumfer-

A pot should be about one-third the height of the plant/ container combination.

a place to pot up

A few years ago, my husband, Greg, made me one of my best birthday presents ever—a potting table complete with running water. While potting up, inspecting, and pruning your houseplants can be performed on a kitchen table or counter, a good potting table makes indoor gardening more enjoyable. When you have all of your tools and materials close at hand, you can quickly and easily perform gardening tasks. You'll find that a well-designed model—one with ample work area, convenient shelves, and numerous drawers—allows you to quickly repot a plant or treat it for pests and diseases. A wide variety of potting tables are available, or you can build your own. When choosing a work space, consider the height you find most comfortable.

ence. If your plant is in a 6-inch pot, the next size up would be an 8-inch pot, and so forth. Avoid choosing a container that is several sizes larger because excess soil around plant roots can become waterlogged and promote fungal disease, which can lead to root rot. It is important, however, to use a pot that will allow the plant to develop a healthy root system. Some plants have shallow roots, while others need more root room. If you feel like the next pot up would be a tight fit, then go up two sizes instead. Containers should also match plants visually. As mentioned previously, the pot should be about one-third the height of the plant/container combination.

There are several types of pots. A standard size pot is best used for plants that are as tall as they are wide, such as dracaenas. Half pots are three-quarters the height of a standard pot and are a good choice for medium-sized plants that require less root space. Bulb pots are shallow and wide and make a good home for succulents and other short-rooted, spreading plants. Hanging pots, which are often plastic but can also be found in clay and ceramic, come in a variety of sizes.

PREPARING TO REPOT

I like to tell my houseplants they'll be getting a new home, and I usually do this when I water them prior to repotting. While our friendly conversation isn't necessary, it's a lot of fun. What is necessary is watering your plants at least two hours before repotting so that they become turgid and ready for the shock of transplanting. Moist soil also makes it easier to remove a plant from its container—a challenging chore when the plant is pot-bound.

repotting essentials

The right tools make the task of repotting your plants easier and more enjoyable. Have supplies near at hand so that you can work as quickly as possible and avoid exposing delicate roots to the air. Gather the following items before repotting:

1. Correct size pot(s)
2. Fine plastic or metal screen to cover drainage holes
3. High-quality organic potting soil (see chapter 2)
4. Plastic container for mixing potting soil
5. Hand trowel
6. Sharp knife
7. Sturdy scissors
8. Plant markers and pencil
9. Water source

THE POTTING UP PROCESS

Step 1

Place plastic or metal screen at the bottom of the pot over the drainage holes. This will prevent soil from leaking onto your floors.

Step 2

Put soil into a plastic mixing container. I like to use restaurant bus trays, which are long and shallow. A bucket will also work. Add organic granular fertilizer, at one-quarter to one-half strength, and vermicompost, if desired. Pour in water and mix well until the soil is moist but not soggy. Wetting makes the soil easier to handle and ensures that the plant gets adequate moisture once repotting is complete.

Step 3

Gently remove the plant from the pot. If it does not come out easily, as happens with some pot-bound plants, hold the plant stem and soil surface steady with one hand and invert the pot with the other. Tap the pot rim against a hard surface. If the plant refuses to budge, run a sharp knife around the inside edge of the pot and try again. If you still have no luck, you have two choices. Cut or break the pot or submerge it in water, allowing it to soak for 20 to 30 minutes. Saturating the plant may finally dislodge it.

indoor gardening the organic way

Carefully remove a houseplant from its pot, making sure to protect the root system.

Step 4

Gently shake the rootball to remove excess potting soil. If you are repotting because of a salt or mineral build-up or to re-establish a healthy pH, gently rinse roots with water. Carefully unwind any circling roots and cut back especially long ones, as well as diseased or broken sections. You can safely cut roots back by 10 to 20%. When the root mass is especially tight and unyielding, slice several times through the sides and bottom. This will stimulate

Repot in a container that is no more than one pot size larger than the previous, that is, no more than two inches greater in circumference.

the roots to grow in the new pot. You may also want to consider dividing the plant (see chapter 10).

Step 5

Place sufficient soil in the bottom of the new pot so that when you set the plant inside, it falls $\frac{1}{2}$-inch to 1 inch below the pot rim. Spread out the roots so they evenly fill the pot and make sure that the plant is centered. Carefully fill in the pot with soil, gently tapping the container every so often as you fill it. This will help prevent air pockets. Continue adding soil until it is level with the rootball and the stem is still exposed. The plant should be sitting at the same

Carefully fill the new pot with soil, gently tapping the container every so often as you fill to prevent air pockets.

level as it was in its original container. Gently press the soil around the stem, making sure that it is even.

Step 6

Using a mixture of water and vitamin B1 (Superthrive or similar product), water the plant well and don't water again until the top inch or two is dry. Overwatering after repotting can quickly lead to fungal disease and root rot. If the soil is still wet but the plant shows signs of wilting, mist the foliage with water. Most plants use less water when they are newly transplanted, so don't be alarmed if your plant doesn't need a drink for some time. Wait at least one month before fertilizing a transplant. Feed only when the plant has re-

staying put

Because of space limitations, you may not want to transplant a large floor plant to a bigger pot. In this case, you can root prune the plant and put it back into the same pot. Root pruning might sound like a harsh way to treat a houseplant, but it's actually a kind way of keeping a plant in check and allowing it to continue to grow in your home. After several years of growth, many large floor plants get tall and may threaten to hit the ceiling. Root pruning allows you to keep a plant at the same size and still maintain its health.

How much you prune will depend on the size of the plant and your goals. If you are trying to get the plant to stop growing and remain in the same size pot, you can remove up to one-third of the old roots with no damage to the plant. Cut away roots with a sharp knife or a small saw, removing the same amount of roots from the sides and bottom of the plant. Try to make clean cuts, as jagged ones can invite disease and decay.

Next, with a pronged hand cultivator, pencil, stake, and/or your fingers, loosen soil from the root ball and discard. This is generally saturated with harmful mineral salts and should be replaced. Doing so also coaxes the roots to grow out into the new soil more quickly.

Root pruning is a good solution for plants that are outgrowing their space.

Before repotting into the same pot, thoroughly clean and rinse the pot to destroy any disease and remove salts. Use a stiff brush and a hot solution of nine parts water and one part bleach. Repot as you would any other plant.

sumed new growth. If you will be moving the plant to a different location, give it a few days to adjust before making the change. Prevent transplant shock by locating it in a space with similar growing conditions.

TOPDRESSING

Reinvigorate plants that you prefer not to repot by top-dressing. This refers to adding compost or potting mix to the soil surface of the container. Scrape away the top two or three inches of soil, taking care not to damage roots. Add a homemade humus-rich mix or pure vermicompost until you reach the same level as the old potting soil. Gently firm down and water. You can add mycorrhizal fungi to the soil at the same time (see chapter 2).

10

adding to your foliage family

Thrifty indoor organic gardeners can easily add to their plant collection without setting foot in a nursery. Don your botanist's hat and perform vegetative propagation, growing new plants from parts of old ones. The offspring you create are clones of the mother plant.

Propagating houseplants offers many benefits. It's inexpensive, allows you to create fresh plants from tired old favorites, is an easy way to replace hard-to-find specimens, and lets you share plants with friends and family. Better yet, a propagated plant from your own stock is already organic and doesn't need to undergo the shock and withdrawal that many nursery-bought plants experience (see chapter 1).

I enjoy the fact that propagated plants are free, but what I really like is playing amateur plant surgeon and creating new life. What other living thing can you duplicate and no one protests? Many precious plants in my collection are there because of propagation. Let me tell you about my wax plant (*Hoya carnosa*).

In the spring of 2004, I accompanied my mother, Lynn, across the country to her birthplace and we researched family history. We located some great-aunts whom she'd never met. One aunt had a lovely wax plant in her dining room window. I admired it, and she said that she got a cutting from her mother over forty years before. When she graciously offered me as many cuttings as I could fit into my suitcase, I took several. Today, my mother and I have our own wax plants. (Mine is pictured in this book's encyclopedia.)

Most houseplants are easy to propagate, which is why they're popular in the first place. Some, like the spider plant, even invite you to make new offspring by providing small, conspicuous plantlets. Springtime, when most houseplants are actively growing and the days are lengthening, is an excellent time to start new plants. You can also successfully propagate in the summer and fall months. During the cold months of winter, your success rate may be low. Though you can't expect instant results with propagation, time and patience eventually reward you with many new houseplants.

There are a variety of ways to propagate. I use five methods in particular to reproduce most indoor plants.

CUTTINGS

The most popular means of creating new plants is to take cuttings and encourage them to form roots. This works well with fleshy stemmed plants, which includes many indoor growers (see list). Two types of cuttings exist—stem cuttings and leaf cuttings.

Stem Cuttings

Here are the steps:

1. Fill a sterile container with moist rooting medium. Tap the container several times to prevent air pockets. Disinfect previously used containers with a one part bleach to nine parts water solution.

2. Using a clean knife or razor blade, remove the top four inches or so of a plant stem that has at least two or three leaf nodes (the point where the leaf attaches to the stem) and no flowers or fruit. Make smooth cuts, as rough ones are subject to rotting. As an extra precaution, sterilize your cutting instrument with the disinfecting solution noted above.

3. Strip off lower leaves, being careful not to touch the surface of the cut with your hands, as this can transmit bacteria and cause the cutting to decay before it has a chance to take root. Once the leaves are stripped, you should have two to three leaf nodes, which are the bumps where you removed the leaves.

4. With a pencil, make a 1-to-2-inch-deep hole in moist rooting medium, depending on the length of the cutting. Insert the cutting into the hole

keeping cuttings humid

To have luck rooting cuttings in soil, it's important to keep them moist and out of drafts until they root. Such conditions can be created by encasing the cutting in a plastic bag that has been secured with a rubber band, or you can use a plastic humidity dome, which I tend to favor.

There are commercial humidity domes (such as those provided with seed-starting kits). Or you can easily make your own from a clean, clear plastic water bottle. Cut the bottom off the water bottle and place over the cuttings. If conditions become too moist in the humidity chamber, take the lid off the water bottle to increase air circulation. Any size water bottle will work, according to the size of your cuttings and their containers. I've used everything from little pints to five-gallon water box bottles.

When temperatures dip below 65°F, cuttings root more slowly and rot is more common. Protect the cuttings and speed up the process by adding bottom heat to the humidity dome, such as a heating pad. Some commercial humidity domes have built-in bottom heat.

created by the pencil, making sure to submerge at least two leaf nodes, which is where roots will emerge. Gently pat soil around the cutting to keep it upright.

5. Keep the cutting moist and in a humidity chamber (see sidebar above) until it roots and then replant. You'll know it's rooted if it puts on new growth or holds firm when you gently tug. (Be careful not to tug too soon or too hard). The amount of time it takes a cutting to root depends on environmental conditions and the type of plant. Some like coleus and pothos are speedy, while other woodier plants can take two

months or more. You'll generally wait three to four weeks.

6. When rooting stem cuttings in water, avoid rot and foul odors by placing charcoal chips at the bottom of the glass. Plants rooted in water can be transplanted when there is a 1-to-3-inch-long root mass.

Leaf Cuttings

A number of fleshy-leaved plants will root successfully from a leaf cutting. With such a cutting, you insert a leaf

Some plants, such as African violets, can be propagated from stem cuttings.

or leaf part into moist soil or water and the leaf roots, often sending out a new side shoot that resembles a miniature leaf.

There are two leaf cutting methods. The first involves removing a healthy mature leaf with the leaf stem (petiole) attached. This is the method of choice for African violets.

The steps:

1. Fill a sterile container with moist rooting medium. Tap container several times to prevent air pockets. Disinfect previously used containers with a one part bleach to nine parts water solution.
2. Remove a healthy, new leaf from the plant, cutting the petiole as close to the base of the plant as possible.
3. Using a pencil or small stick, poke a 1-to-2-inch-deep hole in the moist rooting medium.
4. Into the hole, insert about three-fourths of the petiole. Gently pat the rooting medium around the leaf so that it stands up. Make sure that the leaf doesn't touch the rooting medium.
5. Cover with a humidity dome.

This method also works in water. To get the leaf to stand up, cover the water-filled jar with plastic wrap. Make a thin hole in the plastic with a sharp object. Insert the leaf into the hole, submerging the petiole in water. Because of the water, a humidity dome isn't required.

A second form of leaf propagation involves cutting a leaf

in half horizontally and sticking it into a rooting medium. This is the method of choice for snake plant and radiator plant.

The steps:

1. Fill a sterile container with moist rooting medium. Tap container several times to prevent air pockets. Disinfect previously used containers with a one part bleach to nine parts water solution.

2. Cut the leaf diagonally into 2-to-3-inch-long sections. Let the cut edges dry for several hours. In the case of snake plant, you may have to wait a day or two for it to dry sufficiently, depending on environmental conditions. Wet cuttings will ooze plant juices into the soil and cause rotting.

making rooting medium

For propagation success, it's important to have a good rooting medium. While I advocate using biologically active soil when repotting, in the case of cuttings, a sterile propagation medium is best, as it will help prevent infections that can lead to rooting failure. Over the years, I've devised a rooting blend:

- 1 part washed horticultural sand (allows for drainage and provides bulk)
- 1 part vermiculite (retains moisture)
- 1 part perlite (allows for drainage)
- 1 part peat moss or coconut coir (retains moisture and provides some nutrients)

3. Slide the leaf sections into the rooting medium in the direction of growth. Gently pat the soil around the section.

4. Cover with a humidity dome.

Special Note: When rooting succulents, do so in a mix that is only slightly moist and don't cover with a humidity dome.

AIR LAYERING

This propagation method is best suited for tall, lanky, single-stemmed plants that have become very woody, such as dumb cane, many dracaenas, rubber tree, *Ficus benjamina,* and split-leaf philodendron. Air layering simultaneously serves two purposes: to get a large plant from a single cutting and to prune a plant that has grown too tall. The procedure is a simple one (see diagrams). You partially cut the stem and encourage root formation at that point. Once roots form, you remove the rooted portion and you have a whole new plant, leaving the old stem to grow again.

The steps:

1. Brace the stem, and at the desired location, cut a notch halfway through the stem near a leaf node at an upward slant. Hold the cut open with a toothpick and using a cotton swab, coat with a non-toxic rooting hormone (the only one I

know of is Olivia's Cloning Gel from Worm's Way).

2. Leave the toothpick in and wrap the wound with sphagnum moss that has been pre-moistened with a solution high in phosphorus, such as an organic fertilizer designed for blooming plants or liquid bone-meal.

3. Seal the moss with plastic wrap and secure at the top and bottom with twist ties. (Whenever you work with sphagnum moss, it is important to wear gloves, as moist moss can cause a fungal disease on hands).

4. Keep the interior of the bag moist by spraying when necessary with the organic fertilizer mix or bonemeal solution. In a month or two, the sphagnum should have filled with roots. At that point, cut the stem off below the new roots and pot the new plant. Cut additional stem on the mother plant as necessary to the point of a leaf node. It should eventually branch out from where you make the cut. Dust the exposed cut portion of the mother plant with cinnamon to prevent rotting.

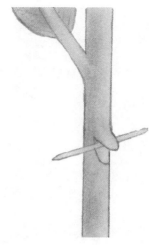

Air layering requires cutting a slit in the stem of a plant and inserting rooting hormone.

Encourage root development in an air layered plant by wrapping the cut in moist sphagnum moss and sealing with a plastic bag.

DIVISION

Some plants can be easily propagated by dividing their roots. This is usually done with plants that grow in clumps or form multiple growing centers that have crowded their pot. Each clump, also known as a crown, is divided into two or more sections and each section is replanted, making a whole new plant.

When a plant can be divided will vary on the type of plant and how large it is. In general, the plant should be well established and have enough of a crown to warrant dividing it two or three times. It is often best done when a plant has become pot-bound, at which point it will readily respond. To determine if a plant would benefit from division, take it out of its pot and remove soil until you can see the root system. If the roots are very dense and there are enough for two plants, divide the root system.

The steps:

1. Take the entire plant out of the container, shake soil off the roots, and examine the plant from the sides, top, and bottom to determine the best location at which to separate. Both parts should have plenty of roots and a healthy growing tip.
2. Some plant roots can be gently tugged apart with your hands or two hand forks. Carefully untangle roots until you have two or more plants. Other plant roots are more closely knit together

and must be cut to separate them. Using a clean, sharp knife, slice starting at the base of the plant and move down through the roots. Be careful to provide each division with adequate roots and always cut out and throw away dead or diseased sections. You should end up with smaller versions of the original plant.

3. Transplant divisions immediately. Water and keep out of direct sunlight until the plants have re-established themselves, at which point they put on new growth. Although they should be kept moist during the adjustment period, be careful not to overwater them.

RUNNERS AND OFFSETS

Some plants create a ready-made plantlet that appears as an appendage of a mother plant. Most of these tiny plants have aerial roots that grow at the end of long shoots. In nature, these small plants will root themselves into surrounding soil or, in the case of orchids, onto trees and other plants. When allowed to root, these miniature plants can be severed from the mother and

Houseplants such as spider plant have runners and offsets that can be rooted in potting medium to create new members of your indoor garden.

will grow into full-sized plants. Spider plant is easily propagated in this way.

The steps:

1. Fill a container large enough to accommodate the offset with moist rooting medium.
2. Using a hairpin or partially opened paperclip, secure the base of the plantlet in the planting medium, keeping it attached to the mother plant.
3. Cover with a humidity dome, if possible. If not, keep the cutting and planting medium moist and place out of direct sunlight and drafts. Mist to increase humidity.
4. In three to four weeks, test the runner by gently tugging to see if it has rooted. If it has, sever it from the mother plant and repot the plantlet in its own pot. Propagation is not an exact science and will require some experimentation. With most plants, you'll have a 75 to 90% success rate. You can make your chances higher by taking cuttings from already healthy plants and from stems that are crisp and turgid. This indicates that the stems have a high concentration of carbohydrates, meaning they have self-contained nourishment and can devote energy to rooting rather than staying alive. Further ensure success by taking two cuttings.

which method for which plant?

Some plants can be rooted by more than one propagation method, while others can only be rooted using one technique.

AIR LAYERING

Croton (*Codiaeum* species)

Dracaena species

Dumbcane (*Dieffenbachia* hybrids)

Ficus benjamina

Rubber tree (*Ficus elastica*)

Schefflera species

Split-leaf philodendron (*Monstera deliciosa*)

DIVISION

African violet (*Saintpaulia* species)

Asparagus fern (*Asparagus densiflorus* 'Sprengeri')

Cast-iron plant (*Aspidistra elatior*)

Chinese evergreen (*Aglaonema modestum*)

Ferns (most)

Ivies (various)

Nerve plant (*Fittonia verschaffeltii*)

Palms (many)

Peace lily (*Spathiphyllum wallisii*)

Peacock/zebra plant (*Calathea zebrina*)

Sedum species

RUNNERS AND OFFSHOOTS

Mother-of-thousands (*Tolmiea menziesii*)

Spider plant (*Chlorophytum comosum*)

Strawberry geranium (*Saxifraga stolonifera*)

STEM CUTTINGS

Anthurium species and hybrids

Arrowhead vine (*Syngonium podophyllum*)

Begonias (many)

Bloodleaf (*Iresine herbstii*)

Coleus x *hybridus*

Croton (*Codiaeum* species)

Dumb cane (*Dieffenbachia* hybrids)

Ficus benjamina

Goldfish plant (*Columnea* species)

Grape ivy (*Cissus rhombifolia*)

Philodendron (*P. scandens*)

Jade (*Crassula ovata*)

Lipstick plant (*Aeschynanthus* species)

Pothos (*Epipremnum aureum*)

Prayer plant (*Maranta leuconeura*)

Purple velvet plant (*Gynura* species)

(continued)

Schefflera species

Swedish ivy (*Plectranthus* species)

Wandering Jew (*Tradescantia zebrina/Zebrina pendula*)

Wax plant (*Hoya carnosa*)

LEAF CUTTINGS

African violet (*Saintpaulia* sp.)

Begonias (some)

Gloxinia (*Sinningia speciosa*)

Radiator plant (*Peperomia* species)

Snake plant (*Sansevieria trifasciata*)

II

clearing the air

Imagine how we'll combat indoor air pollution in the next century. Are you envisioning elaborate space-age machinery controlling what is a top health threat? Chances are you're not thinking of the truth—that nature will provide the cure.

The answer to improving indoor air quality, which the EPA considers two to five times more polluted than outdoor air, is quite simple and logical when you think about it—houseplants. Thanks to over twenty years of research done by NASA and one researcher in particular, we now know that indoor air contains an abundance of volatile organic chemicals (VOCs) harmful to humans and animals and that houseplants not only thrive on those chemicals, they also effectively remove them from the air, making them the perfect addition to the organic home and lifestyle. Renowned scientist Bill Wolverton, Ph.D., author of the internationally acclaimed book, *How to Grow Fresh Air: 50 Houseplants That Purify Your Home or Office,* worked almost 20 years for NASA developing technology that would allow humans to live in a closed environment on the moon or Mars. Through this pioneering research, he discovered that houseplants are the quickest and most effective filters of common, dangerous air pollutants such as formaldehyde, benzene, xylene, and ammonia. All cause a number of ailments such as asthma and allergies and the broader illness now recognized as sick building syndrome. Some, such as benzene (a fossil fuel used as a solvent in the manufacturing of plastic), vinyl chloride, and trichloroethylene (used in dry cleaning), have also been found to cause cancer.

Even humans create indoor air pollution when we breathe. Bioeffluents released during respiration, such as ethyl alcohol, acetone, methyl alcohol, and ethyl acetate, all contribute to poor indoor air quality. And this is just scratching the surface. The truth is, not all indoor air pollutants have been identified. There are probably many more unknown harmful substances lurking in indoor air. Our best bet is to zap them with houseplants.

During their research, Wolverton and his colleagues put houseplants to the ultimate test when they placed them in sealed chambers and exposed them to hundreds of chemicals. By doing so, they found that plants literally suck chemicals out of the air. Considering that plants are the only organisms that add oxygen to the air—everything else uses it up—it's not all that surprising that plants are the answer.

Houseplants clean indoor air in two ways. They absorb pollutants into their leaves and transmit the toxins to

Houseplants work constantly to scour indoor air of harmful toxins.

their roots, where they are transformed into a source of food for the plant. And they emit water vapors, which creates a pumping action that pulls dirty air down around the plant's roots where it is once again converted into food for the plant.

The air-cleaning ability of houseplants is especially needed in office buildings where sick building syndrome is common, thanks to the toxic cocktail served up by office machinery and pressboard furniture—all within insulated buildings that re-circulate air. For this reason, it's a good idea to have a houseplant on your desk within what Wolverton calls your "personal breathing zone," an area of 6 to 8 cubic feet where you spend several hours on a regular basis.

In the home it's good to have a plant near the bed. Plants placed within a personal breathing zone can add humidity, remove bioeffluents and chemical toxins, and suppress airborne microbes like mold. The closer the plant is to you, the better. Even in large open rooms, a plant within your personal breathing zone really improves the air you breathe.

There are many common houseplants that do a great job of cleaning indoor air. Some plants specialize in removing certain toxins. Boston fern, for instance, does the best job of scouring formaldehyde from the air. This especially dangerous chemical is found in most synthetic products, such as particle board furniture, paint, carpeting, and pesticides (though hopefully the latter aren't a part of your gardening arsenal; see chapter 8). This hazardous irritant is believed to cause a condition known as multiple chemical hypersensitivity in some individuals, which leads to asthma and allergies.

The peace lily does a good job of removing acetone, which is found in nail polish remover and various solvents and is particularly drying to the skin.

If plants are so efficient at cleaning indoor air, why don't we all know? Unfortunately, some allergists have unwittingly spread misinformation about houseplants creating airborne mold and mildew. Plants don't give off mold spores; soil does. Houseplants actually reduce mold spores and bacteria by releasing phytochemicals. Research shows that plant-filled rooms contain 50 to 60% fewer airborne molds and bacteria than rooms without plants. As they transpire, plants also humidify the air, which helps soothe nose and throat membranes in some sensitive individuals. I'm an asthma and allergy sufferer, and I know that plants help me considerably. In those areas where I have more plants, I have fewer symptoms. And whenever I travel to a hotel room or another home where plants are not present, my asthma kicks up and my nasal membranes become dry and inflamed.

For those who wish to avoid soil altogether, there are a few solutions to this problem, including growing hydroponically (see chapter 3). You can also cut down on airborne mold spores by covering the soil of your plants with a 1-inch layer of stones, pebbles, or marbles, which will prevent the spores from traveling into the air.

TEN SUPER AIR CLEANERS

Many common houseplants make great indoor air cleaners. In his book *How to Grow Fresh Air*, Wolverton identifies the top fifty plants for cleaning air, rating them on their ability to remove chemical vapors, their transpiration rate, how easy they are to grow, and how resistant they are to pests.

Some plants are better at filtering air and transpiring than others, but don't let that discourage you, says Wolverton, who I have interviewed on several occasions. "If your favorite plant is lower on the list, then just put more of them in your house and office." Following are ten plants from his top fifty list.

Areca Palm (*Chrysalidocarpus lutescens*): This graceful, palm is Wolverton's top pick. It ranks high in removing xylene and toluene from the air.

Boston Fern (*Nephrolepis exaltata*): This plant leads the pack when it comes to eliminating formaldehyde from the home. It also does a good job of extracting other chemical vapors.

Dracaena 'Janet Craig': This is one of the best plants for removing trichloroethylene. It also tops the list for fighting formaldehyde. It's able to reach ten feet tall—give it a few years to grow and it will really clean up your air.

English Ivy (*Hedera helix*): A vigorous climber, this plant ranks high in the removal of formaldehyde and other chemical vapors. It makes a great topiary.

Lady Palm (*Rhapis excelsa*): Considered number two in improving indoor air quality, this tropical plant is number one in disposing of airborne ammonia. It also does a good job of scouring the air of formaldehyde.

Peace Lily (*Spathiphyllum wallisii*): This pretty plant with its tropical white flowers excels in removing a number of toxins, including acetone, methyl alcohol, ethyl acetate, ammonia, benzene, trichloroethylene, and formaldehyde.

Pothos (*Epipremnum aureum*): While this ubiquitous vine isn't at the top of the list when it comes to removal of chemical vapors, it still does its share. It's so easy to grow that you can have them all over your house—like I do!

Rubber plant (*Ficus elastica*): Number four in the top ten, this plant is especially good at cleaning the air of formaldehyde. It is a stately plant with large, round, rubbery leaves and can grow to eight feet or taller. The bigger the plant, the more air it can clean.

Schefflera **species**: One of the easiest large indoor plants to grow, this does an excellent job of extracting a host of chemical vapors from the air. The standard variety can get large, becoming an air-cleaning powerhouse.

Spider plant (*Chlorophytum comosum*): This perennially popular houseplant was given world-wide attention in 1984 when NASA first released research showing its ability to clean the air. It has been shown to remove formaldehyde, as well as many other pollutants.

12

the organic growing difference

Indoor growing can add such pleasure to your life. While you enjoy tending your own little ecosystem and giving your houseplants the best organic care possible, they reward you with lush, vibrant foliage and stunning blooms. You can deeply breathe the air in your home knowing that your houseplants have efficiently cleaned it for you. Using organic pest control and fertilizer also means no qualms about eating edible crops like citrus and herbs.

Gardening organically, your powers of observation become more acute as you look for early signs of pest and disease or notice that a plant is responding well to a worm castings mulch. You come to know each plant and what makes it thrive. And as they grow, you understand how important it is that your plants eat as pure a diet as you do.

Natural gardening also opens you up to the world around you and makes you think about things like beneficial insects, the power of worms, and the birthplace of many of your plants—the jungles of South America. It's also comforting to know that you and your ecosystem are helping to save the ozone layer.

SHARING THE PLANT WORLD WITH KIDS

Once you understand the rhythm of gardening organically indoors, it's easy to share its secrets with friends and family. Considering that children are growing and evolving, introducing them to organic gardening indoors seems fitting. Studies have found that children and adults are calmer and more open to learning when they're surrounded by plants. By showing children that living a pure and natural life is important even for houseplants, you teach them to be kind and gentle stewards of plants and our planet for future generations.

As a mother of three children, I know that both kids and plants fill a room with energy, which is why they're good for one another. Having lived with a house full of plants all their lives, my kids crave them in their space. My daughter, Sabrina, is the official family propagator. She can get anything to grow, and her bedroom is bursting with blooming plants. When she passed her treehouse on to her younger twin brothers, Danny and Jeremy, I painted the space green at their request. Then Jeremy hung his nature-inspired artwork and my husband, Greg, added a TV set. After choosing beanbag chairs for the small space, my sons outfitted themselves in their new digs and Danny announced: "It's got a TV and chairs; now all we need is some plants."

Teaching kids to truly love plants means having them

help with indoor gardening chores. It also means giving them their very own plants—from traditional picks like philodendron and spider plant to more uncommon specialty items like Venus flytrap (*Dionaea muscipula*).

Other unusual plants that kids enjoy growing include the sensitive plant (*Mimosa pudica*). This has ferny leaves that, when touched, fold and droop right before your eyes. Like the prayer plant (*Maranta leuconeura*), the sensitive plant also closes its leaves at night and re-opens them in the morning. Waiting for these plants to fold up can be a great bedtime treat. Growing plants from kitchen scraps such as sweet potatoes, avocado pits, and pineapple tops is another fun project.

KEEPING A GARDEN JOURNAL

One of the most useful garden books you may ever read is your own. Since 1990, I've kept a garden journal. In it, I record information such as when I fertilize, prune, mulch, repot, and acquire plants. For plants that flower and fruit, I jot down when they do so throughout the year. While I could live without my journal and my indoor garden would undoubtedly grow on without it, I often find it useful and interesting to peruse. Your own horticultural records build your awareness of what goes on with your houseplants over time, getting you focused on what you've done and what you still want to do. And if you will be switching from traditional indoor growing to organic methods, a journal can serve as an official record of that transformation.

growing the venus flytrap

Kids are absolutely delighted with the Venus flytrap because it eats insects. Mine was the star of my indoor garden when I was a kid. If you have a sunny windowsill or plant lights, Venus flytraps can be successfully grown indoors.

Light: Provide flytraps with at least two to three hours of sun a day during their growing period from March to October. This usually means an eastern, southern, or western window. If sufficient light isn't available, consider supplemental lighting (see chapter 5).

Dormancy: From November through February, flytraps are dormant. At that time, they require a period of chilling, which can be provided by placing them outdoors in a protected area where they may get frost but won't completely freeze.

Venus flytraps make a fun and intriguing addition to the indoor garden.

Watering: Flytraps require constant moisture. Keep pots sitting in a shallow dish of water low in minerals. Good choices are rainwater, reverse osmosis water, or distilled water. Avoid bottled water unless it is specifically labeled low sodium or purified.

Feeding: Don't fertilize flytraps. They derive nutrients from eating insects. Although they can catch their own prey outdoors, indoors you must provide meals. Sowbugs are a good choice, as well as small spiders, moths, and flies. Avoid hamburger. Feed the prey with tweezers, making sure to hit the tiny trigger hairs within each trap, which will cause it to close on the food. To remain healthy, a plant should have at least one trap feeding at all times. It takes a trap five to seven days to digest a meal.

Repotting: Provide your Venus flytrap with new digs every January. Use a soil mix of two-thirds sphagnum peat moss and one-third perlite or horticultural sand.

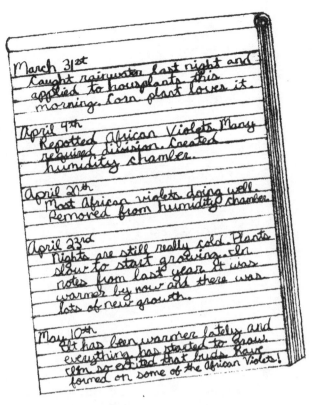

A journal gives you an invaluable record of your indoor gardening experience.

Take the time to start a garden journal, and you'll probably find it has immeasurable benefits. These invaluable gardening tools help you learn from your successes and mistakes. They also take the burden off overworked memories. No need to remember what organic fertilizer you used on your African violets to make them bloom profusely—your garden journal will tell you all about it.

Don't let starting a garden journal intimidate you. Nothing fancy is required. You actually want your garden journal dirty; otherwise, it's like a cookbook without splatters. Entries can be as simple or elaborate as you want. A brief note about how the low light and short days of January are affecting your houseplants will give you important information in years to come.

On April 15, 2003, I wrote: Repotted both bird of paradise in organic potting soil with additional pumice and worm castings. Plants were root-bound—happy to get out of cramped pots. May 28, 2003: Bird of paradise showing signs of being established. They look ecstatic and ready for summer!

On January 15, 2004, I wrote: Blasted mealybugs on arrowhead vine with alcohol spray. Will do another spraying in two days. Those furry, white creatures are so annoying!

Some things to include in your own garden journal:

- Information on work you've done in the garden, including planting, seeding, fertilizing, mulching, and pruning.
- Vital statistics on plants you're growing—height, spread, foliage characteristics, flower color, and blooming season. Pictures of plants and how they look under ideal conditions.
- Basic information about your indoor garden such as light exposure, drafty areas, and ceiling height.
- Plants that perform well for you and those that don't.
- Information on plants seen in other indoor gardens that you want to grow and tips from other gardeners on growing them.

- Records of pest and disease damage, including when it occurs and on what plants. Information on effective treatments and when you apply them.
- Light conditions, including how they change throughout the seasons and any areas that require supplemental lighting.
- Notes from garden books and lectures; magazine and newspaper clippings.
- Indoor gardening plans and tasks you wish to accomplish. Plants you'd like to acquire.
- A diagram of your indoor garden or of the garden of your dreams. Pictures of indoor gardens you admire.
- Photos of your own garden as it progresses, including good and bad times.
- Information on plant suppliers.
- Virtually anything about the garden that pops into your mind on any given day, including a brief mention of how pleased you are with a certain plant's growth.

HOUSEPLANTS AS OLD FRIENDS

Perhaps best of all, gardening organically brings you in tune with your plants, and makes you realize that you're actually in it together. We tend not to give plants the same respect we give animals, but they're living, growing, breathing beings as well. If we have a houseplant for a

seasonal garden chores

A well-planned indoor garden tends to run smoothly. In order to efficiently care for your houseplants, keep this list of quarterly chores on hand in your garden journal.

Winter
- Check for pests; treat if necessary
- Apply beneficial nematodes
- Give plants a shower; thoroughly dry
- Groom, removing dead foliage
- Check that lighting is adequate; adjust if necessary

Summer
- Check for pests; treat if necessary
- Give plants a shower; thoroughly dry
- Groom and prune
- Repot or topdress
- Fertilize

Spring
- Check for pests; treat if necessary
- Apply beneficial nematodes
- Give plants a shower; thoroughly dry
- Groom and prune to stimulate new growth
- Repot or topdress
- Fertilize

Fall
- Check for pests; treat if necessary
- Give plants a shower; thoroughly dry
- Groom
- Repot or topdress
- Fertilize

period of time, we can't help but consider it an integral part of our home. Plants bought at a certain time of our lives serve as a constant reminder of happy or even difficult times. The corn plant (*Dracaena fragrans* 'Massangeana') in my living room always brings a smile to my face. I bought it at just two feet tall in 1987 when I moved into my home. Today, it's over ten feet tall, reaching for the ceiling in my living room and reminding me of many happy years. As you care for your indoor garden, you begin to see that getting plants to grow the distance and thrive for years is not that difficult, and it's so rewarding.

13

the plants

An eye-catching indoor garden is diverse. Besides foliage plants, add a vertical element with trailers and climbers and tall and large specimens and put the finishing touches on your houseplant showcase with flowering beauties. Just for fun, throw in some edible crops.

FOLIAGE PLANTS

Foliage plants comprise the backbone of the indoor garden. While they come in a huge variety of green tones—from pale to nearly black—many flaunt foliage in bright colors like red, yellow, and orange. Such head-turners are often variegated, which refers to irregular coloration in the form of blotches, speckles, stripes, and swirls on the same leaf. Sometimes these multi-color designs are a result of a genetic mutation, which a smart propagator picked up on and duplicated, while at other times it's simply how the plant was originally found in the wild. Some striking examples of this phenomenon are the polka-dot plant, which has medium-green leaves that are spotted with vibrant pink, red, or white. The peacock plant is another good example. This eye-catching plant has satin-textured, deep green olive-striped leaves with veins of yellow-green and purple undersides that resemble a peacock's tail. It is especially striking when hit by light.

Considering the wide array of green and variegated foliage available and the immense variety of leaf shapes, sizes, and textures, it's possible to find a plant that will match any color and design scheme in your home. As a matter of fact, going to the nursery is a lot like browsing through wall covering and upholstery samples. The choices are nearly limitless. Many houseplants have colorful foliage and rich textures that give you plenty of decorating opportunities. Coleus, for instance, has velvety leaves that come in shades of red, green, white, pink, and yellow.

Some green foliage plants can tolerate low light, but variegated members of the houseplant family often require medium to bright light to keep their colors from fading. Even green plants suffer when lighting is too low.

Croton (*Codiaeum* species)

The brilliant, colorful leaves of this houseplant make it a must-have in any indoor garden. Where other foliage plants fade into the background, croton stands out. With its variegated, patterned leaves in yellow, green, and red, and sometimes pink and white, it can be worked into just about any decor. The waxy, often leathery, leaves vary in shape, size, and variegation, depending on the cultivar. Some leaves can get as big as one foot long, and others have a stippled and corkscrew effect.

While not the easiest indoor plant to grow, crotons can be enjoyed in the indoor garden if you keep a few things in mind.

The eye-catching, variegated leaves of croton come in yellow, green, and red and sometimes pink and white.

Care Guidelines

- Keep evenly moist. Although they can tolerate drying out occasionally, it is best to keep crotons well watered.
- Provide ample humidity. Crotons are native to the Malay Peninsula and Pacific Islands and thrive on moist, warm air. Grow on a humidity tray, mist frequently, and group with other plants. Also try to keep temperatures from dropping below 60°F. Keep away from windows in the winter months.
- Place in bright light. Crotons do best in high light. When conditions are dim, leaf color fades. Give two to three hours of bright light each day, making sure the entire plant gets covered. They enjoy an unobstructed eastern exposure.

- Other tips: Provide crotons with a rich, well-drained acidic potting soil that has a pH of about 6.5. Fertilize two to three times per year. Also be aware that they don't respond well to change in light or temperature, which can cause foliage drop. Avoid shock in large plants by topdressing instead of repotting.
- Warning: Crotons are members of the euphorbia family, which tend to have toxic sap that will permanently stain clothing.

VINES AND CLIMBERS

Eye-catching indoor gardens capitalize on the verticality offered by vining and climbing plants. By growing plants that cascade and creep, you invite the eye up, creating interest and a feeling of being surrounded by greenery. Hanging also enables some plants to grow as nature intended. Houseplants like wandering Jew and spider plant look their best when they take to the air.

Sufficient lighting is one of the most important aspects of growing vertically indoors (see chapter 5). Signs that a hanging or climbing plant is not getting enough light include weak, leggy growth, leaf drop, and insect infestation. Too much light shows up on leaves in the form of burned and scorched spots.

Providing stability is critical in the vertical garden. Hanging baskets tend to be very heavy when wet, so make certain that the hook is firmly anchored in the ceiling and that the plant is supported by a sturdy chain or heavy cord. Choose hanging locations carefully. Avoid areas where the container can be easily bumped. Although there are ceramic baskets for hanging, lighter weight plastic tends to be a safer choice, especially for large plants.

Heat rises, and plants up high can dry out quickly. Many need to be watered once a week—some even more often. When it's time to water, the easiest and cleanest method is to take the plant down and soak it in the sink, allowing it to drain well before re-hanging. (After they drain in the sink, I place mine on old towels until the pot bottom is dry).

Regular pinching and pruning keeps vines and climbers looking full and lush (see chapter 7). Trim unhealthy leaves—they are unattractive and rob the plant of energy. Root cuttings and plant them in the same container to give an even bushier look; make sure to repot when a vine or climber has become root-bound.

Pothos (*Epipremnum aureum*)

The easy-to-grow pothos is an often overlooked vining houseplant that is a great addition to any indoor garden. It goes almost dry before protesting, and I've even seen this rugged vine survive for weeks without a drop of water. A few years ago, my son Jeremy's second grade teacher gave me her pothos after explaining that every summer it went into a state of dormancy when no one watered it. Each fall, after a few waterings, it always came back to life, but she decided that I'd make a better parent.

Pothos is probably the easiest of all vining houseplants to grow.

Few indoor plants will climb as readily and as far as pothos. Take advantage of the plant's eagerness and train it to grow across a wall by attaching the vine to small hooks or inconspicuous nails. Let it spill from entertainment centers, bookcases, and high window ledges. Train it up a trellis, moss poll, or staircase.

Pothos thrives in small pots for years and requires very little, if any, fertilizer. It rarely gets pests or diseases, is easy to propagate, and can be grown in just about any lighting situation.

Care Guidelines

- Avoid overwatering. Pothos do best when you let them approach dryness and then drench them. They communicate when they want water by flagging, which refers to the point before wilting when a plant's leaves appear slightly limp and lose their sheen.
- Fertilize occasionally. Pothos will probably do just fine without fertilizer, but the plant will be happier and grow more vigorously with some food. Feed with a dilute mix of an organic fertilizer two or three times a year.

indoor gardening the organic way

- Consider lighting. Pothos will grow in just about any lighting situation, although it's important to note that the variegation may fade some when the plant is exposed to very bright or dim lighting conditions. Medium light is ideal.
- Prune. Without some pinching, pothos tend to grow single-stemmed and become lanky. Occasionally pinch tips to encourage bushy growth.
- Propagate. Pothos reproduce easily from stem cuttings in soil or water. Root cuttings for entirely new plants or use them in existing containers. Or for an even faster and easier way to fill in bare spots in containers, each time you prune, insert the cuttings directly into the same pot. Just remember to keep these new cuttings moist at the point of contact with the soil until they become rooted and established.

LARGE AND TALL PLANTS

Large and tall plants are a great way to add height and sheer presence to a room. While smaller plants act as accessories, large plants enliven a space and make a statement.

They may seem challenging, but large floor plants are fairly easy to grow. The corn plant and other dracaenas like 'Janet Craig' (*D. deremensis*) and *D. Marginata* thrive in most interiors. *Schefflera* is another easy-to-grow favorite, as are many palm trees.

Choose plants wisely. Many large floor plants take years

to grow and therefore require a financial investment on your part. Depending on their size and the type of plant, they can range from $30 to $200. Considering the cost involved, it's important to choose a healthy plant (see chapter 1).

Use caution when transporting. If care is not taken, irreversible damage can be done to a large floor plant on the ride home (see chapter 1). Lay it on its side for transporting and never grasp a plant by its trunk, which can break off roots. Always lift the plant by the container.

The biggest problem with tall indoor timber is outgrowing your home. Once they approach the maximum height and size your house allows, fertilize only as necessary. You can also keep growth in check by root pruning or top-dressing (see chapter 9), both of which will ensure continued health. And when pruning becomes necessary, air layering is often your best bet (see chapter 10).

Because tall floor plants tend to stay put for watering, it's a good idea to leach them every six months (see chapter 3). You can do that where the plant is, using a turkey baster to empty the cachepot, or move it outdoors or into the shower. Drench well to remove toxic soluble salt build up.

Split-Leaf Philodendron (*Monstera deliciosa*)

I have many favorite houseplants, but split-leaf philodendron is at the top of the list. This plant always reminds me of those snowflakes we all made in elementary school by folding the paper and cutting. This indoor garden gem is also aptly called the Swiss cheese plant. Its leaves become dissected with deep splits and perforated with oval holes. *M. Deliciosa*'s striking heart-shaped foliage, along with its easy-to-grow, vigorous nature, make it an eye-catching focal point. It is a fast-growing climbing plant that will reach—in ideal indoor conditions—ten to fifteen feet high and eight feet across. In its native habitat, the jungles of Central America, split-leaf philodendron grows up into the rainforest canopy, climbing as high as seventy feet. It attaches itself to the trunks and branches of other trees with long tentacle-like aerial roots.

The large heart-shaped foliage of the split-leaf philodendron becomes dissected with slits and holes when the plant receives adequate light.

Although it rarely fruits indoors, *M. deliciosa* lives up to its name by producing a cone-like fruit, which is actually an unripened flower spike. The fruit matures in about a year, and the taste is described as a combination of banana, pineapple, and mango. It should be eaten only when ripe; unripe fruit will irritate the mouth and throat.

Care Guidelines

- Provide medium to bright light, but no direct sun. Plants in lower light tend to produce smaller leaves without splits or holes.

- Water and fertilize frequently. *M. deliciosa* has a big appetite. Water when the soil approaches dryness and feed monthly. Younger split-leaf philodendrons require frequent repotting as they grow. Topdress when more mature specimens reach the desired size.

- Provide humidity when necessary. Although it is a jungle plant, split-leaf does tolerate low humidity better than many plants. If your home is especially dry, however, place the plant over a humidity tray. They also love misting.

- Other tips: The split-leaf philodendron has cord-like aerial roots that emerge from the base of the plant. In its native habitat, it uses these roots to climb trees and absorb nutrients. These aerial roots can be trained to climb a support, such as a moss pole (see chapter 7), or they can be directed into the soil. Prune some out when there are many.

FLOWERING BEAUTIES

Few things are more delightful than a long-lasting indoor living bouquet. They may seem difficult to grow indoors, but given the right lighting conditions and nutrient-rich organic food, many flowering plants can be kept in bloom with very little effort. *Anthurium* species and hybrids are a good example. They look exotic, but they can flower most of the year.

For even further fun, try growing fragrant indoor

plants. Research has shown that pleasant aromas alter mood, calming and cheering us. The selection of scented indoor bloomers is limited, but there are a surprising number of plants that will naturally perfume your house throughout the year such as various begonias, wax plant, jasmines (*Jasminum sambac* 'Maid of Orleans' is terrific), and *Murraya paniculata* 'Orange Jasmine,' a waxy white flower that emits an intense orange-blossom fragrance.

The number one secret to getting most houseplants to bloom is proper light. Without sufficient light, they can't produce flowers. Most houseplants need indirect, bright light to bloom. The morning sun found in an eastern window is often ideal. African violets are an exception. They require a bright, unobstructed northern exposure. Southern locations also work for many bloomers, though they may require protection from the sun by sheer curtains or adjustable blinds. Right in front of exposed western windows tends to be too hot, but when sheer curtains or blinds are used, flowering plants can do well there. (See chapter 5 for more details on lighting.) Flowering plants that don't get enough light will stop blooming and elongate or grow very slowly, while those that get too much light will have scorched and yellow leaves and may also stop flowering.

Blooming houseplants require fertilizer on a regular basis, in addition to healthy organic soil. Phosphorus is key in promoting budding and blooming. Choose a fertilizer that is designed to promote flowering and is highest in this key nutrient (the middle number), or provide your plants with additional phosphorus by using liquid bonemeal or soft rock

phosphate. Watering is also important for successful flowering. Droughted plants are likely to drop flowers and buds.

African Violet (*Saintpaulia* species)

When my daughter, Sabrina, and I saw our first African
violet at the nursery, we were hooked—but skeptical. The
stunning purple blooms were sure to light up the house,
but would the plant re-flower? To our delight, it blooms
constantly, as do the many others now in our collection.

Grow an African violet, and you'll soon discover why
they're considered one of the most popular flowering
houseplants. Give them the right conditions and you can
enjoy their pert, happy blooms throughout the year.

African violet flowers come in a variety of striking colors, including purple, pink, mauve, lavender, white, cran-
berry, coral, and blue. Some blooms are variegated. Flowers
are single, semi-double, or double and are often ruffled or
fringed. Leaves are fuzzy and gen-
erally oval-shaped, and some are
variegated.

Discovered in eastern Africa
in 1892 by an amateur horticul-
turist, Baron von St. Paul-Illaire,
African violets have been enjoyed
by indoor gardeners for over
100 years. A governor of the
area's Usambara District at the
time, St. Paul-Illaire spotted a

African violets can bloom all year indoors.

indoor gardening the organic way

small plant with blue-purple flowers and gathered seeds and specimens. The plant material ended up at Berlin's Royal Botanic Garden, where the director grew plants from the seeds and then identified a new plant genus—*Saintpaulia ionantha*—named after the man who discovered them. Although African violets resemble viola flowers, they are actually in the Gesneriaceae family.

The secret to getting African violets to look their best and re-bloom is giving them the right growing conditions, which are similar to our preferred living environment.

Care Guidelines

- Monitor indoor temperatures and humidity. African violets do best at 70 to 75°F and approximately 60% humidity. Provide humidity trays and group plants (see chapter 6).
- Give proper lighting. African violets like bright, indirect light. Provide eight to twelve hours of sunlight or artificial light per day. Make sure sunlight isn't too bright, or it will burn leaves and inhibit flowering. A well lit northern exposure window is an ideal location. I have such a situation in my dining room, which is where I bud up all of my African violets before putting them in other areas of the house, such as Sabrina's room. Once they stop blooming, I return them to the dining room window and start the cycle again. If you have no northern exposure windows, make sure to

protect plants in other locations with blinds or sheer curtains. Keep in mind that African violets also require eight hours of daily darkness, so turn off artificial lights at night.

- Watch watering. Keep African violets evenly moist but not overly wet. Watering methods that avoid wetting the leaves are preferred, such as bottom watering or wicking (see chapter 3).
- Other tips: Feed African violets on a regular basis and repot every six to twelve months. Watch out for pests such as mealybugs, which like to congregate on old flowers. Pinch spent blooms regularly.

SUCCULENTS AND CACTUS

Succulents, and cactus specifically, lend a Southwestern flair to any room. They grow well indoors, as long as you provide adequate light and water them properly. Succulents tend to sport striking foliage that comes in a wide variety of variegated colors and many shapes and sizes, while cacti have bristles. Both flower.

Although many cacti and succulents struggle indoors because of high light requirements, some will thrive, such as jade (*Crassula ovata*), snake plant (*Sansevieria trifasciata*), *aloe vera*, barrel cactus (*Echinocactus grusonii*), Christmas cactus (*Schlumbergera* species), Easter cactus (*Rhipsalidopsis gaertneri*), hens and chicks (*Echeveria elegans*), oldman cactus (*Cephalocereus senilis*), and rat-tail cactus (*Aporocactus* species).

Cactus and succulents will soak up as much light as you

give them and do well in southern or western windows. Water when they get dry, but don't wait too long. Drought tolerant doesn't mean no water at all. They also require monthly feeding during the spring and summer months.

EDIBLE INDOOR PLANTS

Not many plants will fruit indoors without a lot of fuss, but some varieties of citrus (Meyer lemon and calamondin orange) and various herbs can be successfully grown indoors.

I like to think of growing edible crops as a fun experiment. Even when the harvest is minimal, I'm so excited to eat something from my indoor garden. And when it comes to herbs, you usually only need a sprig or two.

All edibles will need some direct light each day or they won't produce well. Citrus requires light to fruit and herbs need it to grow dense foliage. Both crops can live in front of a western or southern window, although watch for leaf burn and move plants back if that occurs. Citrus and herbs also thrive under artificial lighting, especially HID systems (see chapter 5).

When growing citrus indoors, it's important to choose a dwarf or even bonsai tree. Such specimens have been bred to stay compact and are more likely to fruit indoors. Proper nutrients are critical to the success of any indoor fruit tree. Make sure that your fertilizer has trace elements, such as iron, magnesium, and zinc (see chapter 4). It's also important to be patient. Many fruit trees will take from six months to a year to produce an edible fruit once they flower. Some citrus will bloom year-round indoors if they're happy, but they tend to have their heaviest bloom in spring.

To get citrus trees to fruit indoors, it's important that you act as a bee and hand-pollinate your tree. This should be done with any indoor crop that produces a fruit or a vegetable. To hand pollinate, stick a small paintbrush inside of each flower, gently wiggle the brush and then move on to another bud and do the same. This ensures that you mix pollen from male and female flowers, which triggers fruit production.

Herbs grown indoors should be pinched regularly to keep them bushy and healthy. Always remove blooms from annual herbs like basil because flowering will negatively affect leaf production and can change the flavor of the herb. Keep in mind that this herb can only be grown in the spring and summer months, while some perennial herbs like rosemary can be grown indoors year-round. Other suitable herbs for indoor growing include chervil, chives, marjoram, mint, oregano, parsley, sage, and thyme.

online resources

Charley's Greenhouse & Garden
www.charleysgreenhouse.com
Catering to greenhouse growers, this company has a variety of useful items, such as lighting systems, meters (for pH, moisture, and light), hydroponic growing supplies, root stimulants, propagation supplies, indoor hoses, self-watering systems, and potting benches.

Dr. Earth
www.drearth.com
For years this forward-thinking company has produced organic, biologically active soils and fertilizers containing mycorrhizal fungi and other beneficial soil microbes. They also carry organic insecticidal sprays.

EB Stone
www.ebstone.org
Here you'll find biologically active soil that includes mycorrhizal fungi and humic acids. They also carry organic fertil-

izers, including liquid fish emulsion and kelp meal, and some organic pesticides.

GardeningZone.com
www.gardeningzone.com

This company carries a wide variety of beneficial insects for the indoor garden, as well as composting worms.

Healthy Houseplants.com
www.healthyhouseplants.com

An informative website covering all aspects of gardening indoors organically. There are articles on houseplant care, as well as features on new developments in indoor gardening, and a plant encyclopedia.

Plant'It Earth
www.plantitearth.com

This all-organic resource carries a wide variety of indoor garden products, including fertilizers and pest control, root stimulants, natural rooting hormone, soil additives such as pumice, hydroponic growing mediums and supplies, indoor lighting systems, and tools such as moisture and pH meters.

Rincon-Vitova Insectaries
www.rinconvitova.com

This company has many beneficial insects for the indoor garden.

TerraCycle

www.terracycle.net

This innovative company carries an all-purpose plant food made from liquefied worm compost. The convenient, ready-to-use spray is great for foliar feeding, and it's even packaged in recycled soda bottles.

Worm's Way

www.wormsway.com

As its name implies, this company carries worm castings, as well as worm farm supplies. They are also a good source for other organic fertilizers, including compost tea, hydroponic growing supplies, and HID lighting systems.

index

disease: bacterial, 8, 104, 116; benefits of, 97, 98; checking for, 105–6; controlling, 105–6, 114–18; neem oil as treatment, 101–2; result of mistreatment in retail establishments, 6, 7; role of soil, 14; signs of, 9, 105, 114–18; spread among newly acquired plants, 4, 6, 105

distilled water, 26, 43

dividing, 128

dolomite lime, 26, 28, 29

Dr. Earth, 181

dracaena: container choice, 124; corn plant (*Dracaena fragrans* 'Massangeana'), 162, **203**; *Dracaena cragii* compacta 'Janet Craig,' 152, 171, **203**; *Dracaena marginata*, 80, 171; *Dracaena marginata* 'Tricolor,' **204**; leaf spot on, 116; lighting for, 4, 62; pH, 24; propagating, 145; pruning, 88

drycleaning, 148

dumb cane (*Dieffenbachia* hybrids), 62, 88, 90, 116, 145, **200**

Easter cactus (*Rhipsalidopsis gaertneri*), 178

EB Stone, 181

Echeveria elegans. See hens and chicks

Echinocactus grusonii. See barrel cactus

ecosystem, 155–56

edible crops, 155, 165, 179–80

Eisenia fetida (red worm), 19

Encarsia formosa (parasitic wasp), 113

English ivy (*Hedera helix*), 152

EPA, 147

Epipremnum aureum. See pothos

Epsom salts (magnesium sulfate), 50, 51

ethyl acetate, 148

ethyl alcohol, 148, 152

euphorbia, 168

exotics. *See* unusual houseplants

expanded clay, 43

feather meal, 27, 50

fern: fertilizing, 54; and humidity, 70; lighting for, 62, 67; pH, 24; propagating, 145; soil mix for, 27, 29

fertilizer, 45–54; build-up, 44; burn, 54, 115; for citrus, 179; conversion to usable food, 14; for flowering plants, 54, 175; frequency/timing of feeding, 53, 162; with humic acid/humus, 18; importance of feeding houseplants, 46; liquid versus granular, 51; to maintain height and size, 172; N-P-K ratio and nutrient roles explained, 47–48; plant spikes, 52; after repotting, 129, 131; role of soil, 14; for sick/weak plants, 54; signs that houseplants need feeding, 46, 47; in specialty soil mixes, 29; worm compost, 17, 21. *See also* chemical fertilizer; organic fertilizer

Ficus benjamina (weeping fig), 4, 24, 63, 90, 145, **204**; lighting for, 4, 140

Ficus elastica. See rubber tree

Ficus lyrata. See fiddle-leaf fig

Ficus pumila. See creeping fig

fiddle-leaf fig (*Ficus lyrata*), 62, 80, **204**

firecracker flower (*Crossandra infundibuliformis*), 62, **205**

fish emulsion, 50

fish meal, 27, 50

Fittonia verschaffelti. See nerve plant

Hedera helix. See English ivy
Hedera helix 'California.' *See*
  California ivy
hens and chicks (*Echeveria elegans*),
  178
herbs, 155, 179–80
horticulturists, ix
*How to Grow Fresh Air: 50 Houseplants
  That Purify Your Home or Office,* 147
humic acid. *See* humus
humidity: air temperature effect
  on, 71; decreasing for pest
  control, 116–17; definition
  of, 70, 71; dome/chamber,
  136; excessive, 81, 116;
  geography/location effect on,
  71, 72; in greenhouses, 1;
  grouping to create, 77;
  importance to houseplant
  health, 69, 70; increasing for
  pest control, 111; measuring
  humidity, 72; misting, 73–75,
  116–17, 174; for newly
  acquired plants, 4; optimum
  levels for health, 71;
  placement effect on, 72, 77,
  80; plants requiring high humidity, 70; plants requiring
  low humidity, 80; raising,
  150–51; relative humidity, 71;
  terrariums, 78, 79; and tip
  burn, 115; trays, 4, 75–77,
  80; and watering, 41;
  weather's effect on, 71–73
humus (humic acid), 14–18;
  homemade humus-rich soil
  mix, 28; mulching to
  increase, 15; in organic fertilizer, 18, 49, 50, 51;
  stabilizing pH, 26; and soil
  type, 36
hydroponics, 43, 44, 151
hygrometer, 72, 76, 81

Hypoaspis (fungus gnat mite), 108
Hypoestes phyllostachya. See polka-dot
  plant

insecticidal soap, 84, 100–101,
  107, 110–11, 113
Internet plant sources. *See* mail-
  order
Iresine. See bloodleaf
iron, 48, 51, 52, 179
iron deficiency. *See* chlorosis
ivy, 145

jade (*Crassula ovata*), 145, 178, **200**
Jasminum sambac 'Maid of Orleans,'
  175
journal, garden, 157, 159–61
jungle, 69, 155, 173

kelp meal, 50

lacewings (green), 107
ladybug (ladybird beetle), 99,
  107, 114
lady palm (*Rhapis excelsa*), 152, **204**
large and tall floor plants, 165,
  171–74, 186, **203–5**
leaching: of newly acquired
  plants, 3; to remove chemical
  fertilizers, 3, 44, 54; to
  remove soluble salts, 3, 40,
  41, 43, 44, 122; for tall and
  large floor plants, 172
leaf mold, 27
leaf node, 87, 141
leaf problems: burn/scorch, 3,
  43, 54, 57, 61, 63, 168;
  chlorosis, 9; curling, 9, 63,
  70, 105; distortion, 8, 63,
  105; drooping/wilting, 8, 63,
  105, 110, 115; drop, 3, 11, 70,
  110–11, 168; fungus, 8, 101,
  104, 115, 117; loss, 61, 105;

Murraya paniculata 'Orange Jasmine,' 175

mycorrhizal fungi, 21–23; adding when topdressing, 131; application of, 23; benefits/ importance of, 21, 22; fertilizer and, 22, 23; history of, 22; houseplant's natural dependence on, 21; orchids and, 22; potting soils/ products containing, 21–23

NASA, 147–48, 153

neem oil (BioNeem), 101–2, 113, 117

nematodes (beneficial), 108, 162

Neoseiulus californicus, 112

Nephrolepis exaltata 'Bostoniensis.' See Boston fern

Nephrolepis exaltata 'Can Can.' See Can Can fern

nerve plant (*Fittonia verschaffeltii*), 62, 79, 88, 145, **200**

nitric acid, 44

nitrogen, 24, 54; results of deficiency, 47; role of, 47

N-P-K, 47–49. See also fertilizer

nutrient deficiency: signs of, 9, 46–49, 52

offsets. See runners

oil, horticultural, 102, 104, 110–11, 113, 117

oldman cactus (*Cephalocereus senilis*), 178

Olivia's cloning gel, 141

orchid: and container type, 36, 121; fertilizing, 54; lighting for, 63; and mycorrhizal fungi, 22; potting soil mix, 27, 29; runners, 143

organic fertilizer: benefits to houseplants, 3, 44, 46; frequency, timing of feeding, 53, 54; as a "health food" diet, 46; identifying and choosing, 49–52; positive effect on soil, 46; types, 50; use when air layering, 141; use when repotting, 126. See also fertilizer

organic gardening, ix, x, 98, 155, 157

organic lifestyle, ix, 98

Orius insidiosis (minute pirate bug), 113

oxygen, 148

oyster shell, 26, 50

Pacific Islands, 167

palms, 24, 62, 145, 171

parlor palm (*Chamaedorea elegans*), 79, **204**

peace lily (*Spathiphyllum wallisii*), **206**; air-cleaning ability of, 150, 152; lighting for, 62; propagating, 145; pruning, 89

peacock plant (*Calathea zebrina*), 62, 145, 166, **200**

peat moss, 17, 27–29, 36, 79, 139

Peperomia species. See radiator plant

perlite, 26, 27–29, 36, 79, 139, 158

peroxide rinse, 116

pesticides/insecticides: chemical, ix, 98, 99, 103, 150; organic, 101, 103–4, 107, 110–11, 113

pests: and beneficial insects, 99, 100, 162; benefits of, 97, 98; causes, 83; checking for, 9, 105, 106, 155, 162; insufficient light, 168; organic/non-toxic treatments for, 100–114; as result of

encyclopedia of plants

The secret to growing a lush indoor garden is nurturing plants that readily withstand the vagaries of indoor life. I've seen many books that encourage readers to grow a variety of outdoor and very tropical plants indoors. While I'm sure that someone, somewhere can grow such plants, I'm not including them in this encyclopedia. The following are true houseplants that can be grown indoors by anyone, anywhere for an extended period of time. Some of these plants are more particular than others, but all generally survive in the indoor garden. Give them the organic treatment and they'll thrive.

This is not to say that I discourage growing exotics indoors. I have several. Just try specialty plants in limited doses. Master growing one before trying another.

For ease of use, the plants listed here are divided into specific categories: Foliage Plants, Vines and Climbers, Large and Tall Plants, and Flowering Beauties. Soil mixes noted can be found in chapter 2. In terms of pH for soils, acidic refers to a reading of 6.00–6.50, neutral is 7.00, and alkaline refers to a reading of 7.00–7.50. See chapter 5 regarding lighting intensity.

Asparagus Fern (*Asparagus densiflorus* 'Sprengeri')

Light: Medium to bright
Moisture: Water when soil surface dries
Humidity: 50–80%
Soil: Fern mix
Fertilize: Spring/Fall
Care: Easy
pH: Acidic

Bird's Nest Fern (*Asplenium nidus*)

Light: Medium to bright
Moisture: Keep soil evenly moist
Humidity: 50–80%
Soil: Fern mix
Fertilize: Spring/Fall
Care: Moderate
pH: Acidic

Cast-Iron Plant (Aspidistra elatior)

Light: Low to medium
Moisture: Water when soil is almost dry
Humidity: 30–70%
Soil: Humus-rich mix; extra perlite or pumice
Fertilize: Spring/Fall
Care: Easy
pH: Neutral

Chinese Evergreen (*Aglaonema modestum*)

Light: Low to medium
Moisture: Water when soil surface dries
Humidity: 50–80%
Soil: Humus-rich mix
Fertilize: Spring/Fall
Care: Easy
pH: Neutral

Coleus (*Coleus* × *hybridus*)

Light: Medium to bright
Moisture: Keep soil evenly moist
Humidity: 60–80%
Soil: Humus-rich mix
Fertilize: Spring/Summer
Care: Moderate
pH: Neutral

Croton (*Codiaeum* species)

Light: Medium to bright
Moisture: Keep soil evenly moist
Humidity: 60–90%
Soil: Humus-rich mix
Fertilize: Year-round
Care: Moderate to challenging
pH: Acidic

Dumb Cane (*Dieffenbachia* hybrids)

Light: Medium
Moisture: Water when soil surface dries
Humidity: 50–70%

Soil: Humus-rich mix
Fertilize: Year-round
Care: Easy to moderate
pH: Neutral

Jade (*Crassula ovata*)

Light: Bright
Moisture: Water when soil is almost dry
Humidity: 30–50%

Soil: Cactus/succulent mix
Fertilize: Spring/Summer
Care: Easy to moderate
pH: Alkaline

Maidenhair Fern (*Adiantum* species)

Light: Medium
Moisture: Keep soil evenly moist
Humidity: 60–90%
Soil: Fern mix

Fertilize: Year-round
Care: Moderate to challenging
pH: Acidic

Nerve Plant (*Fittonia verschaffeltii*)

Light: Medium
Moisture: Keep soil evenly moist
Humidity: 60–90%

Soil: Humus-rich mix
Fertilize: Year-round
Care: Moderate
pH: Neutral

Peacock Plant (*Calathea zebrina*)

Light: Medium to bright
Moisture: Keep soil evenly moist
Humidity: 60–80%

Soil: Humus-rich mix
Fertilize: Spring/Fall
Care: Moderate
pH: Neutral

Polka-Dot Plant (*Hypoestes phyllostachya*)

Light: Medium to bright
Moisture: Water when soil surface dries
Humidity: 40–60%
Soil: Humus-rich mix

Fertilize: Year-round
Care: Easy
pH: Neutral

Prayer Plant (*Maranta leuconeura*)

Light: Medium
Moisture: Keep soil evenly
Hu

Soil: Humus-rich mix
Fertilize: Year-round

Purple Velvet Plant (*Gynura* species)

Light: Medium to bright
Moisture: Keep soil evenly
moist
idity: 60–80%

Soil: Humus-rich mix
Fertilize: Year-round
Care: Easy-moderate
pH: Acidic to neutral

Radiator Plant (*Peperomia* species)

Light: Low to medium
Moisture: Water when soil
is almost dry
Humidity: 50–80%

Soil: Humus-rich mix
Fertilize: Year-round
Care: Easy
pH: Neutral

Snake Plant (*Sansevieria trifasciata*)

Light: Low to bright
Moisture: Water when soil
is almost dry
Humidity: 20–50%

Soil: Cactus/succulent mix
Fertilize: Spring/Fall
Care: Easy
pH: Alkaline

Arrowhead Vine (*Syngonium podophyllum*)

Light: Low to medium
Moisture: Water when soil
surface dries
Humidity: 40–70%

Soil: Humus-rich mix
Fertilize: Year-round
Care: Easy
pH: Neutral

Boston Fern (*Nephrolepis exaltata* 'Bostoniensis')

Light: Medium to bright
Moisture: Keep soil evenly
moist
Humidity: 60–80%

Soil: Fern mix
Fertilize: Year-round
Care: Moderate
pH: Acidic

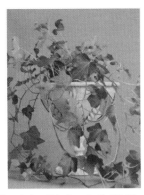

California Ivy (*Hedera helix* 'California')

Light: Medium to bright
Moisture: Water when soil
  surface dries
Humidity: 40–60%

Soil: Humus-rich mix
Fertilize: Spring/Summer
Care: Easy
pH: Neutral to alkaline

Can Can Fern (*Nephrolepis exaltata* 'Can Can')

Light: Medium to bright
Moisture: Keep soil evenly
  moist
Humidity: 50–80%

Soil: Fern mix
Fertilize: Year-round
Care: Moderate
pH: Acidic

Creeping Fig (*Ficus pumila*)

Light: Medium
Moisture: Water when soil
  surface dries
Humidity: 50–80%

Soil: Humus-rich mix
Fertilize: Spring/Summer
Care: Easy to moderate
pH: Neutral to alkaline

Grape Ivy (*Cissus rhombifolia*)

Light: Medium to bright
Moisture: Water when soil
  surface dries
Humidity: 40–60%

Soil: Humus-rich mix
Fertilize: Spring/Summer
Care: Easy
pH: Neutral

Philodendron (*P. scandens*)

Light: Low to medium
Moisture: Water when soil
  surface dries
Humidity: 40–70%

Soil: Humus-rich mix
Fertilize: Year-round
Care: Easy
pH: Acidic to neutral

Pothos (*Epipremnum aureum*)

Light: Low to bright
Moisture: Water when soil
  is almost dry
Humidity: 40–80%

Soil: Humus-rich mix
Fertilize: Year-round
Care: Easy
pH: Neutral

Spider Plant (*Chlorophytum comosum*)

Light: Medium to bright
Moisture: Water when soil
is almost dry
Humidity: 30–60%
Soil: Humus-rich mix
Fertilize: Spring/Fall
Care: Easy
pH: Acidic to neutral

Wandering Jew (*Tradescantia zebrina/Zebrina pendula*)

Light: Medium to bright
Moisture: Water when soil
surface dries
Humidity: 40–60%
Soil: Humus-rich mix
Fertilize: Year-round
Care: Easy
pH: Neutral

Wax Plant (*Hoya carnosa*)

Light: Bright
Moisture: Water when soil
surface dries
Humidity: 40–70%
Soil: Humus-rich mix
Fertilize: Spring/Summer
Care: Easy
pH: Neutral to alkaline

Corn Plant (*Dracaena fragrans* 'Massangeana')

Light: Medium
Moisture: Water when soil
surface dries
Humidity: 50–70%
Soil: Humus-rich mix
Fertilize: Spring/Fall
Care: Easy
pH: Alkaline

Ctenanthe

Light: Medium to bright
Moisture: Keep soil evenly
moist
Humidity: 60–80%
Soil: Humus-rich mix
Fertilize: Spring/Fall
Care: Moderate
pH: Neutral

Dracaena cragii compacta 'Janet Craig'

Light: Medium
Moisture: Water when soil
surface dries
Humidity: 40–60%
Soil: Humus-rich mix
Fertilize: Year-round
Care: Easy
pH: Neutral to alkaline

Dracaena marginata 'Tricolor'

Light: Medium to bright
Moisture: Water when soil
surface dries
Humidity: 40–60%

Soil: Humus-rich mix
Fertilize: Year-round
Care: Easy
pH: Neutral to alkaline

Ficus benjamina (commonly called Weeping Fig)

Light: Bright
Moisture: Water when soil
is almost dry
Humidity: 40–70%

Soil: Humus-rich mix
Fertilize: Every other month
Care: Easy
pH: Neutral to alkaline

Fiddle-leaf Fig (Ficus lyrata)

Light: Medium to bright
Moisture: Water when soil
surface dries
Humidity: 50–70%

Soil: Humus-rich mix
Fertilize: Spring/Fall
Care: Easy to moderate
pH: Neutral to alkaline

Lady Palm (Rhaphis excelsa)

Light: Medium
Moisture: Water when soil
surface dries
Humidity: 50–80%

Soil: Cactus mix
Fertilize: Spring/Summer
Care: Moderate
pH: Neutral to alkaline

Parlor Palm (Chamaedorea elegans/Neanthe bella)

Light: Medium to bright
Moisture: Water when soil
is almost dry
Humidity: 40–80%

Soil: Humus-rich mix
Fertilize: Year-round
Care: Easy
pH: Neutral to alkaline

Rubber Tree (Ficus elastica)

Light: Medium to bright
Moisture: Water when soil
is almost dry
Humidity: 40–70%

Soil: Humus-rich mix
Fertilize: Spring/Fall
Care: Easy
pH: Neutral to alkaline

Schefflera species (commonly called Umbrella Plant)

Light: Medium to bright
Moisture: Water when soil surface dries
Humidity: 50–80%

Soil: Humus-rich mix
Fertilize: Year-round
Care: Easy
pH: Acidic to neutral

Split-leaf Philodendron (*Monstera deliciosa*)

Light: Medium to bright
Moisture: Water when soil surface dries
Humidity: 40–70%

Soil: Humus-rich mix
Fertilize: Year-round
Care: Easy
pH: Acidic to neutral

African Violet (*Saintpaulia* species)

Light: Medium
Moisture: Keep soil evenly moist
Humidity: 60–80%
Soil: Blooming mix

Fertilize: Year-round
Care: Moderate to challenging
pH: Acidic to neutral

Anthurium species and hybrids

Light: Medium to bright
Moisture: Water when soil surface dries
Humidity: 60–80%
Soil: Blooming mix

Fertilize: Spring/Fall
Care: Moderate to challenging
pH: Neutral to alkaline

Begonia (*Reiger hybrid/B.* × *hiemalis*)

Light: Medium to bright
Moisture: Keep soil evenly moist
Humidity: 60–80%
Soil: Blooming mix

Fertilize: Spring/Fall
Care: Moderate to challenging
pH: Acidic to neutral

Firecracker Flower (*Crossandra infundibuliformis*)

Light: Medium to bright
Moisture: Keep soil evenly moist
Humidity: 60–80%

Soil: Blooming mix
Fertilize: Spring/Fall
Care: Moderate
pH: Neutral

Gloxinia (*Sinningia* speciosa)

Light: Medium
Moisture: Keep soil evenly
moist
Humidity: 70–90%
Soil: Blooming mix

Fertilize: Year-round
Care: Moderate to
challenging
pH: Acidic

Goldfish Plant (*Columnea* species)

Light: Medium to bright
Moisture: Keep soil evenly
moist
Humidity: 60–85%

Soil: Blooming mix
Fertilize: Year-round
Care: Easy
pH: Neutral

Lipstick Plant (*Aeschynanthus* species)

Light: Medium to bright
Moisture: Keep soil evenly
moist
Humidity: 50–80%
Soil: Blooming mix

Fertilize: Year-round
Care: Moderate to
challenging
pH: Neutral

Moth Orchid (*Phalaenopsis* species)

Light: Bright
Moisture: Water when
bark medium dries
Humidity: 60–80%
Soil: Orchid bark or
pumice with one-part
vermicompost

Fertilize: Year-round
Care: Easy to moderate
pH: Acidic to neutral

Peace Lily (*Spathiphyllum wallisii*)

Light: Low to medium
Moisture: Water when soil
surface dries
Humidity: 40–60%

Soil: Blooming mix
Fertilize: Year-round
Care: Easy
pH: Neutral

Zebra Plant (*Aphelandra squarrosa*)

Light: Bright
Moisture: Keep soil evenly
moist
Humidity: 70–90%
Soil: Blooming mix

Fertilize: Year-round
Care: Moderate to
challenging
pH: Acidic to neutral